ACKNOWLEDGMENT

The author expresses his appreciation to Mr. Warren Lehman, Assistant Dean of the Law School at Washington University, St. Louis, Missouri, for his valuable assistance in the preparation of the manuscript.

This book is affectionately dedicated to my wife, Barbara, and to Noma and William Copley.

THE LAW OF
Art &
Antiques

By
SCOTT HODES

Member, Illinois and District of Columbia Bars

A PRIMER
FOR ARTISTS
AND COLLECTORS

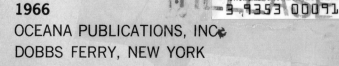
1966
OCEANA PUBLICATIONS, INC.
DOBBS FERRY, NEW YORK

56

The Legal Almanac Series brings you the law on various subjects in non-technical language. These books do not take the place of your attorney's advice, but they can introduce you to your legal rights and responsibilities.

CONTENTS

FORWORD by Harold Haydon ix

INTRODUCTION xiii

PART I: THE ARTIST

Chapter I SELLING ART WORKS 1
Commissions To Produce 1
 Death of Patron or Artist 5
Sale Through a Dealer 6
Sale Through Art Rental Outlets 9
Mediation and Arbitration 10
Codes of Ethics 11

Chapter II COPYRIGHT 13
History of Copyright Legislation 13
What Can be Copyrighted 14
 Copyright or Patent 16
Who Can Secure a Copyright 16
Legal Protection Offered by Copyright 18
What Constitutes an Infringement 18
 Fair Use 20
 Non-Copyrightable Works 21
How to Secure a Copyright 22
When is a Work Published 24
Transfer of a Copyright 26
Protection of Titles 27
The Moral Right Doctrine 28
International Copyright 29
Conclusion 30

Chapter III INVASION OF PRIVACY, LIBEL,
DISPARAGEMENT, UNFAIR COM-
PETITION AND IMITATION 31
Invasion of Privacy 32
Libel 34
Disparagement 37
Unfair Competition 37
Imitation in Art 38
Conclusion 39

Chapter IV   THE ARTIST AND INCOME TAXES 41

Averaging Income—"Spreading Back" 41
"Spreading Forward" 44
Donating Art to Charity 45
Deductibility of Expenses 47
Prizes and Awards 49
Foreign Artist Earning Income in the
United States 49
United States Citizens Earning
Income Abroad 51

PART II: THE COLLECTOR

Chapter V   PURCHASING ORIGINAL ART 53
Auctions 55
Legal Mechanics of an Auction 56
Warranties at Auctions 58
Specific Performances as a Remedy
for Failure to Deliver 59
Duty of Auctioneer to Seller 60
Auctions and the Uniform Com-
mercial Code 61
Purchase from a Gallery or Private Person 61
Rental Arrangements 63
Purchasing from the Artist 64
Syndications 65

Chapter VI   CUSTOMS 67
Original Works 70
Prints and Graphic Arts 70
Work of Art Produced by an American
Artist Residing Temporarily Abroad 72
Antiques 72
Stained Glass Windows and Tapestries 73
Intended Use 73
Export Restrictions 74
General Customs Provisions 74
Declaration for Customs 74

Chapter VII TAX AND THE COLLECTOR 77
Capital Gains on the Sale of Art 77
Donation of Art Works 80
Valuing a Work of Art 81
Gift of a Future Right to Possess 82
Limitations on Charitable Donations 82
Contributions in Installments 83
Conclusion 84

Chapter VIII INSURANCE 85
Insurance as a Contract 85
The Formation of an Insurance Contract .. 86
Subject Matter of the Insurance Contract .. 87
Types of Insurance Policies 87
Art Works on Exhibition or Loan 90
Loss or Destruction of Art Work 91

EPILOGUE 93

APPENDICES 95

I.   Contracts entered into between Henri Matisse and Bernheim-Jeune.
II.   Artist-Dealer Form of Contract: The Artists Equity Association.
III. Code of Ethics: The Artists Equity Association.
IV.   Code of Fair Practice: The Artists Guild.
V.   Agreement for Sale of Painting, with Reservation of Copyright.
VI.   Assignment of Copyright in a Painting.
VII. Model Release.
VIII. List of Hans van Meegeren Art Forgeries.
IX.   Conditions of Sale—Parke-Bernet Galleries, New York.
X.   Rental Agreement—Washington Gallery of Modern Art.

FOREWORD

This concise volume, growing out of years of work, is a most welcome and timely herald of awakening American interest in the fine arts. It must be a truism that any really serious human undertaking is soon codified and then relies on law to define its scope and defend its rights. As art bulks larger in the American consciousness, it progressively loses the frivolous mein imposed on it by our Puritan heritage and acquires dignity and honor that demands for it full and equal rights with other life-enhancing activity.

A review of the interrelations of art and the law over the centuries would show that commitments to produce art, to acquire art, to donate art, and to establish property rights in art often have led to legal action. The accounts of that action have contributed extensively to our knowledge of art history. Indeed, one may assume that most major works of art become a matter of public record through transactions of a legal nature that bring them into being. And while there are some hilarious pages in the record when artist and critic, or artist and patron, have clashed in court, and some humiliating passages when blundering officials attempted unsuccessfully to distinguish works of fine art from mundane materials, most of the record is solid and constructive. It provides a sound basis for resolving present and future problems.

One may take for granted that when millionaire dealers and patrons transact business in art their legal interests and problems are cared for adequately. One cannot safely assume as much for the artist, however, for his knowledge and resources ordinarily are meager. Too often he is the victim of his own special combination of ignorance of the law, generosity, and pride. This book is a shield for him.

The collector also needs guidance along the pitfall-paths of purchasing, importing, lending, and giving works of art, lest his innocent largesse reap troubles with tax collectors and customs officials. This book may be his salvation.

It is a mistake to think that anything about fine art is trivial, for even worthless art is capable of exploitation, so great is popular esteem for art if not for artists. The painter or sculptor working at his trade may have no thought except for the sheer joy of creation, yet in effect he is creating his estate and its value to him and his heirs will depend upon how clearly he understands, or even senses, his rights and responsibilities. If he no more than senses them, in all probability he can find competent counsel, for I have noticed how the prestige and public status of art, together with its highly personal complications of taste and judgment, attract the best legal minds.

Although the author has confined himself in this book to the most general problems arising from sales, commissions, copyright, taxes, customs, and insurance, he has regularly summarized and interpreted the law to reveal its nature and intention. Accordingly, the imaginative reader will have no difficulty in seeing beyond usual horizons prescribed by habit and everyday experience. In a world of expanding media of communication, art remains the best all-around means of communication, and so it behooves the artist and the collector of his work to look over the horizon to future opportunities and hazards.

But, whatever the future may bring, the present holds problems enough in which this book can prove its usefulness. The traditional stereotype of the artist who is quite incompetent in business matters belongs to the present as well as to the past. How grateful this one is to the disreputable dealer who robs him; how angry and helpless that one who worked months on a portrait only to have it refused without payment; how stricken that other when costs of a commission ran higher than his fee! Too often the artist finds that he has traded his work for a puff of fame, yet even that satisfaction can be combined with tangible rewards if the artist knows his legal rights.

Nor is the art collector, although a businessman, likely to foresee in the specialized world of art all contingencies of acquiring, protecting, and conveying to others his artistic treasures. This book can aid him too. Here is one unhappily trying to satisfy the tax collector who thinks all of a painter's work must be of equal value regardless of date. There is another caught in the mills of customs and import regulations. This one learned too late of an advantageous way of giving his collection to the public. And that one paid for a forgery before seeking authentication.

To these beleaguered artists and collectors, and even more to their able associates whose common sense is often a reliable guide, this book is addressed. It is comprehensive and imaginative enough to contain some fresh fact, insight, or suggestion for everyone. Its great charm is that it discusses the law in layman's language, is not cluttered with references to cases, and frequently points out that some matters are so special in their circumstances and so complex in ramifications that professional legal counsel should be sought. This is not a sue-them-yourself lawbook, but is instead the lucid exposition by a good legal mind of common or typical problems created by conflicting interests in the field of art, together with possible remedies.

Possibly the greatest contribution the book can make is in the training of young artists in the art schools of America. I recall that not so long ago students, in their search for expression, were allowed to neglect basic technique until their disintegrating pictures literally became a scandal. Now the schools are teaching the fundamentals of sound technique. Yet, in my judgment it is far more scandalous to send young artists into the professional world with only the sketchiest knowledge of the ethics and business practices of art. I hope that our schools everywhere will require study of the legal aspects of the artist's profession, for which a book such as this one is an essential resource.

Scott Hodes, the author, a graduate of the University of Chicago, has had a personal interest in art since undergraduate days and an exceptional opportunity to live with and abet the growth of a private art collection. His efforts will be especially welcomed by all those artists who have been striving to give status to their profession through codes of ethics, standard contract forms, and similar instruments, some of which are reproduced in the Appendices. Equally, collectors will applaud and benefit from up-to-date information on government regulations as well as basic law affecting purchasing, customs, taxes, and insurance in the field of art. Indeed, anyone interested in the arts and their coming of age will find this valuable little book both fascinating and instructive.

The University of Chicago   Harold Haydon
October, 1965

INTRODUCTION

This book is an invitation to the artist and the collector to consider some of the legal ramifications involved in being an artist or being a collector. This discussion is designed for the layman, but it is not intended as a guide to being your own lawyer. Rather the book is intended to help the reader recognize when he has a legal problem and to communicate enough of the flavor of the law that he will be able to understand and work effectively with legal counsel. The author recognizes that the law, like art itself, may elude and confuse the uninitiated. If the flavor of the law has been lost or distorted in translation, the author must take full responsibility.

PART I

THE ARTIST

Chapter 1

SELLING ART WORKS

I suppose that every serious artist expects to earn a decent living from his work. This is nothing to be ashamed of; an artist does not have to work in a drafty attic just to prove to the world that he is dedicated to his art. This does not mean, however, that an artist may not have to forego certain economic benefits while awaiting public acceptance. But every artist has a right, and even a duty to himself and his art, to attempt to sell his creations.

For better or for worse, selling a work of art projects the artist into the realm of business and law. A sale may be consummated in a variety of ways. The artist may choose to sell his work directly to a purchaser who intends to put the object in his own home; he may sell through a dealer or gallery; he may sell a finished work, or he may produce a work to meet certain specifications or tastes. But every arrangement presents different legal problems. The purpose of this chapter is to examine types of transactions artists are likely to enter and to warn against possible pitfalls.

Commissions to Produce.

A commission is an agreement to purchase a work of art that does not yet exist, but which the artist promises to bring into being. It is generally negotiated by the artist directly with his patron. The fact that the work does not exist when the agreement is reached causes most of the legal problems an artist is likely to encounter in accepting a commission. What if his patron is not satisfied and refuses to pay?

If the patron is not to be satisfied, his pronouncement is not likely to come until the artist has almost completed his work. But what happens at this point will depend on the original agreement, or contract. The die was cast long before.

Operationally, a contract may be defined as an agreement that will be enforced by a court of law. To be enforceable a contract must be founded on "consideration" (something of value to be given or done in exchange for something of value to be given or done by another). The law does not ordinarily force a person to keep a promise if he does not receive something in return; the theory is that there must be an exchange to support a contract. Illustratively, a promise to paint a picture for a person is not binding unless that person promises something of value (money or the like) in return. Generally, two acts are needed to create a contract. The first is an offer—"I will give you this, if you will give me that." The second is an acceptance—"Agreed."

An infinite variety of conditions or qualifications may be made a part of any contract. "This agreement is void in the event of a strike," or "if delivery is not made within thirty days," or "if I am not satisfied with the product," are terms frequently used. Satisfaction of the patron is a clause common to many artistic commissions, and it can be a very troublesome one for the artist.

The general policy of the law is to allow people to make any kind of contract they want to, and to enforce that contract as written. This policy goes so far as to permit the making of contracts by which the duty of a party to perform his part of the bargain depends solely upon the state of his own mind—his own satisfaction. Therefore, if an artist enters a contract by the terms of which it is clear that the patron is to pay only if he is satisfied, the artist can collect only if he is able to achieve satisfaction on the part of his patron.

A person's state of mind is, of course, very hard to prove. Satisfaction is a state of mind. It is possible that a patron, having suffered a loss in the stock market, will decide that he wants to breach a contract and that he will feign dissatisfaction to avoid the appearance of a breach. It may be possible to convince a court that the dissatisfaction is feigned, but it will not be easy to do. If an artist makes this type of contract, he should be aware of the possible consequences.

Whether the artist finds himself completely at the mercy of his patron's whim may depend upon how the personal taste and satisfaction clause is written. If the contract says the artist shall be paid if he produces a "satisfactory" picture, the effect may be different than if the contract recites that the patron need pay only "if he is satisfied." Some courts may hold that a satisfactory picture is one that is objectively satisfactory; that is, one that would satisfy a reasonable man. In that event, proof of quality might be made by the expert testimony of other artists or of art dealers. However, most courts will interpret satisfaction clauses to require that the product satisfy the purchaser, unless it is completely unambiguous that the standard intended was the satisfaction of a reasonable man. The assumption is made, on the basis of general observations about human nature, that satisfaction of the purchaser is probably what was intended.

When working under a personal satisfaction contract, the artist should specify that his patron pay specified portions of the contract price at various stages of the creative process. Where this is not acceptable, the artist may gain some protection by having the patron put his initials on drafts, designs and preliminary sketches, indicating that he is satisfied at various steps of the creative process. Then should the patron show reluctance to accept the final product, there is at least some evidence available from which it may be argued that the patron's dissatisfaction is not genuine.

If a dissatisfied patron cancels his contract, the artist will usually be entitled to dispose of the work elsewhere, unless it is a mural in the patron's house, of course. A portrait, however, presents a special problem. It may be an invasion of the patron's privacy, or even a form of libel if the subject is portrayed in a derogatory light, to sell or exhibit a portrait without authorization. If a portrait just cannot be completed to the patron's satisfaction, the artist may choose to hide or destroy his work, or he may swallow his pride and renegotiate the contract at a lower price. The only other possible choice is to obtain a written release from the subject permitting exhibition or sale.

If the reader will refer back to the sample "satisfaction" clauses discussed earlier, he will note that they were so phrased that they made the patron's duty to pay contingent on satisfaction. They did not promise satisfaction. If the artist says, "I will paint a satisfactory picture in return for so much money," he has promised to satisfy. Where that is true, a failure to satisfy will be a breach of contract by the artist, though generally one with only minor consequences. Little damage has been done the patron except perhaps to waste some of his time. However, there may be fairly serious damage if the work of art is attached to the property of the patron. The patron may sustain costs in removing the unsatisfactory work, and to get what he wanted he may be required to hire another artist at a higher price. In that case, damage may be assessable to the artist if he promised to satisfy. If the work of art will be affixed to the patron's property, it is especially important for the artist to use the contingent form, rather than the promissory form.

Where the work of art is a mural or becomes affixed in the house of the patron, the patron cannot retain the benefits of the artist's work, while at the same time refusing to pay. This is true even if the patron is not satisfied.

4

There is a rule of law against unjust enrichment. In a situation of this nature, the artist is not entitled to receive his contract price because he did not fulfill his end of the bargain; however, he is entitled to a sum of money which adequately represents the value of his work. Theoretically, and as a practical matter too, the value of the artist's work should be less than the contract price since the original contract contemplated not only a work of a certain value, but one that corresponded exactly to what the patron wanted. That satisfaction should have some monetary equivalent over and above the value of the work on the open market.

DEATH OF PATRON OR ARTIST: The contract between an artist and his patron is called a personal service contract. The patron is contracting for the services of a particular artist, and substitutes are not acceptable. This type of contract must be distinguished from one in which A contracts to give B's house a coat of paint. If A gets sick and cannot do the work himself, he may elect to find another painter to finish the job. B has no right to object because it makes little difference who does house painting, so long as he is reasonably competent. But a man who hires Jackson Pollack is not likely to be satisfied if he gets a Norman Rockwell. And generally, the rights and duties under a personal service contract terminate with death or disability of either party, as would be expected.

In the absence of any language to the contrary in the contract, if performance by the promisor (artist) becomes impossible by virtue of death, insanity, or disabling illness, the contract is discharged, and the artist or his estate will be under no obligation. Likewise, if the work of art is a portrait, the patron or his estate will be under no obligation if the subject, either the patron or a third person, dies before there have been any sittings. If sittings are completed, however, so that the artist can finish the painting without the subject, the patron or his estate would be liable for the agreed price. The result would probably be different if the artist had promised to "satisfy" the person who died. In this case, the contract would most likely be discharged for failure of consideration.

The rules discussed in this section are those that would be applied where the contract makes no provision for a contingency such as death, because that contingency was not contemplated when they entered the contract. Courts have rules, based on common sense, to help them guess what the parties to a contract would have wanted in a specific situation had they foreseen that such a situation might arise. Probably the main function of an attorney in the writing of a contract is to help his client to explore possibilities that would not ordinarily occur to the client, to advise the client to decide in advance how these possibilities should be dealt with, and to express the client's position in a manner that will be both clear and legally binding. When that is done, questions are less likely to arise in the first place; and when they do, courts will not have to guess the intentions of the parties. Of course, the parties to a contract may decide to do exactly the opposite of what a court, shooting in the dark, would guess they would want done. As long as the result is not illegal or against public policy, the courts will go along. After all, one of the main doctrines of contract law is that the parties should be free to contract as they choose.

Sale Through a Dealer.

Probably the most popular method of selling art is to locate a dealer who will undertake to publicize and sell the artist's works. The dealer generally sells through gallery showings or exhibitions. In this way, art critics and the public are given an opportunity to see, evaluate, and purchase, the artist's works.

The artist and the art dealer may enter into one of two general arrangements, either of which may be varied in an infinite number of details. Basically, the dealer may purchase art and resell it, or serve as the artist's agent,

6

selling on a commission or fee basis works that are owned, until sale, by the artist. As an example of variations within these two general classes, when the dealer buys he may agree to buy, and the artist promise to sell, the artist's entire output; the dealer may take a certain specified portion; he may have a right of first refusal; or he may just buy an occasional work. Where the dealer contracts to purchase all of the artist's output, the artist is bound by law to sell to the dealer every work he produces. Where the dealer has the right of first refusal only, if the dealer decides not to purchase the artist is free to sell to a third party.

If the paintings continue to belong to the artist while in the hands of the dealer, the dealer is an agent for the artist. In consideration of the dealer's services, the artist generally agrees that the dealer is to receive a commission or a fee. Such agency agreements may stipulate that the dealer is to have the exclusive right to sell the artist's works or that the artist is free to sell himself or through others. The agency relationship is subject to certain fixed legal rules, but an agency is set up by contract, so many of its terms may vary at the will of the parties.

In law, an agent has certain well-defined responsibilities. His fundamental role is to act on behalf of his principal, usually for certain limited and specified purposes. For example, an agent empowered to sell an artist's works would not also have the power to sell the artist's house. But the agent does have the power, as long as the agency relationship exists, to sell a painting, or a sculpture, and the artist cannot interfere when the agent has contracted with a third party to sell one of the artist's works. The artist cannot come in and say, "I don't think you charged enough money for that piece," or "I've decided to keep that painting." In the absence of an agreement to the contrary, the agent (gallery) may bind the principal (artist) to any deal within the scope of the agent's authority.

An artist and a dealer may enter into an agency relationship by a formal, written contract, or by very informal means. For example, an artist may create an agency by leaving his work with the dealer, and it will be assumed that the artist consents to be bound by the contractual arrangements that are normally given by this dealer. Then, too, an agency to procure commission agreements for the artist may arise informally as the result of a stranger indicating that he knows a person who would like to commission the artist. If the artist accepts the commission, he will probably be bound to compensate the volunteer agent at a reasonable rate. Whether the artist leaves his work with the dealer or accepts a commission negotiated by a volunteer agent, the agency relationship, even though informal, may be a continuing one until definite steps are taken to terminate it. Basically, then, it is the artist as principal who is responsible for the creation of the agency relationship. Therefore, if the artist chooses to end the relationship, he must so advise the agent and also serve notice to the public, so that persons who may deal with the agent will not be misled.

The law also dictates that the dealer has certain recognized responsibilities toward the artist. The dealer must remain within the scope of the authority granted to him by the artist. If the artist has specified that certain pieces within the possession of the dealer are not for sale, the dealer must not violate this trust. The dealer cannot purposely sell the artist's work at a cut-rate price to his friends. Likewise, if the dealer fails to exert care for the artist's works that are in his possession, he may be held liable for their market value. Moreover, if the artist has given the dealer an exclusive agency agreement, the dealer must exercise reasonable efforts to publicize and sell the artist's work. Regardless of the type of contract that is negotiated between the artist and the dealer, the artist is not bound to perform unless and until the agent actually exerts some substantial effort on the artist's behalf.

Written contracts have certain advantages over informal agreements. By negotiating and commiting the terms of an agency relationship to writing, each of the parties will

8

avoid many of the difficulties that may arise in the future. Obviously, it is better for the parties to have decided in advance how contingencies are to be handled, than to leave the question to judicial interpretation in a lawsuit. The failure to negotiate a binding contract at the inception of a working relationship has destroyed countless friendships and has consumed untold sums in legal fees and court costs. The contracts entered into between Henri Matisse and his dealer should be examined carefully, as they exhibit considerable ingenuity in solving problems that may well have arisen had Matisse merely left his paintings with a dealer and said, "Please sell them for me." These contracts are reproduced in Appendix I. For comparative purposes a recent Artist-Dealer Form of Contract distributed by the Artists Equity Association is reproduced in Appendix II.

Sale Through Art Rental Outlets.

It has been estimated that there are approximately five hundred art collectors throughout the world who compose the market for high priced objects of art—those works priced at $50,000 or more. While the purchases and sales of these recognized individual art buyers make spectacular news, the art market does not exist on these transactions. As a matter of fact, the art market is not designed for these buyers. The average buyer is interested in works that sell for less than $300.

In an effort to penetrate the real art market and assist the up and coming artist, a museum or gallery will frequently offer an art rental service to its patrons. This service permits the artist to submit works of art in the hope that a collector will rent, and eventually purchase, his work. (Legal problems confronting the collector in this situation are discussed at pages 63 to 64.)

Most contracts executed between an art rental agency and an artist stipulate that the artist shall set the selling price and that the rental agency is entitled to a specified commission or handling charge for its services. Frequently,

9

too, the artist agrees to transport his works to and from the art rental outlet, and assumes responsibility for any loss or damage that may occur in transit. Another provision may recite that the articles will not be cleaned or repaired either by the art rental service, or by the borrower, except with the written permission of the artist. Most rental services also agree to insure all items in their possession, with the understanding that potential liability will not exceed the selling price. As a measure to protect his copyright, the artist should insist that the agreement between the art rental outlet and the borrower specify that works of art will not be photographed, sketched, or otherwise reproduced without the express written consent of the artist.

Any agreement between the artist and rental agency should necessarily provide for termination of the relationship. This is generally effected by written notice from one party to the other. At the time of notification, the artist's works should be removed promptly from possession of the rental agency, unless they are on loan at that time. In this event, the artist should wait until the article is returned by the borrower. Should the borrower exercise his option to purchase the work after the artist-agency agreement is terminated, but before the termination of the lease, the artist may not be entitled to the return of the article.

Over the past ten years, many art museums throughout the United States have opened art rental outlets. This vehicle has enabled the contemporary artist to expose the public to his works. It is of the utmost importance that the artist exercise great care when entering into a relationship with a rental agency; when doubtful about any provisions of their agreement, he is best advised to seek the assistance of a competent attorney.

Mediation and Arbitration.

When an artist and his patron or an artist and his dealer develop a dispute, a third party may be asked to lend his good offices to help solve the problem. This is known as mediation and it in no way binds the respective parties. On the other hand, a dispute may be referred to a third party by mutual agreement of the parties, made either prior to the actual dispute in anticipation of foreseeable difficulty, or after the dispute has arisen. This type of an agreement, known as arbitration, will usually make the decision of the third party binding on the disputants.

When parties wish to have possible disputes settled by arbitration, they may use the services of the American Arbitration Association. The Association maintains panels in more than thirteen hundred cities, and for a nominal fee will supply a panel consisting of two or three Association members, frequently specialists in the field of dispute. The panel will generally conduct an informal hearing before handing down a decision.

Codes of Ethics.

In an effort to bring order out of chaos in the field of art merchandising, codes of ethics have been adopted for the professional artist and for the commercial buyer of artwork by various Associations and Guilds. For the most part, these standards are predicated upon the belief that adherence to a code of fair practice will contribute to the welfare of the artist by establishing and building professional and public respect. The Code of Ethics of The Artists Equity Association is reproduced in Appendix III, and the Code of Fair Practice as formulated by the Joint Ethics Committee of the Society of Illustrators, the Art Directors Club and the Artists Guild is reproduced in Appendix IV. These codes are modified from time to time by formal amendment or as a result of interpretation in hearings before the bodies that administer these Codes.

Chapter 2

COPYRIGHT

An artist, writer, or painter is a social being, and art is a form of communication. The author is probably as much flattered by the number of people who read his book as he is at the size of his royalty check. Likewise, the painter or sculptor whose work is thought worthy of acquisition for public display may receive greater satisfaction from this accomplishment than if the work is acquired by a private collector who alone will receive his message. Some artists, even in this commercial age, will waive any payment for works of art which they may create for public institutions.

Because art is in part a public activity, a myriad of legal problems may arise. As a general rule, the artist does not wish to restrict the legitimate publicity given his talents through photographs, sketches, reproductions, and the like. Yet, the artist properly concerned with earning a livelihood from his work, must protect himself from publicity given for purposes of economic exploitation. How can the artist expose his works to the public, while reserving for himself alone, the rights pertaining to those works? This is the problem that has led to copyright legislation.

History of Copyright Legislation.

Long before the War of Independence, it had been established by the common, or judge-made, law of England that the creator of an intellectual work owned that work just as he did the chair upon which he sat. This ownership or property right, which prevented copying as well as stealing, continued as long as the creator did not expose his work to the public. What rights he had after exposure or publication were, at best, open to question until the enactment of the first copyright legislation in 1710, the Statute of Anne. That statute, upon which all subsequent copyright legislation is based, was enacted in response to pressure from the printing industry, not too long after restrictions on entering the printing business had been lifted. With anyone able to open a printing establishment, there was always the temptation to pirate a competitor's best seller.

The old common law copyright continued to exist even in the presence of a statute, but only until such time as publication was effected. The statutory copyright was available to the creator only after his work was published. This distinction continues in American law. We now have federal copyright legislation applicable once a work has been published, and common law rights, administered by the individual states, respecting works that are still in the possession of their creators.

The modern American copyright law, like the Statute of Anne, gives the owner of the copyright a monopoly to reproduce his work for a period of years. Prevailing American law protects that right for 28 years after the first publication, with the provision that a copyright can be renewed for a second 28 year period. As long as a work remains unpublished, however, the copyright has no time limitation and the property rights in the work may be passed on for generations without losing its common law copyright.

What Can Be Copyrighted.

The power of Congress to enact uniform copyright (and patent) laws was granted by the United States Constitution. Original copyright laws were concerned only with written works, so the Constitution (Article 1, Section 8, Clause 8) provided that "the Congress shall have the

14

power . . . to promote the Progress of Science and useful Arts, by securing for limited Times to Authors and Inventors the exclusive Right to their respective Writings and Discoveries." In implementing this grant of power, Congress rejected the idea of subsidies or patronage as a stimulus to the arts. Instead, economic incentive for our creative citizens was provided in the form of the legal protection accorded by a copyright.

Over the years, the terms *author* and *writing*, as used in the Constitution, were interpreted by the courts of law to include musicians and their music and graphic artists and their works. And before an author could be given a copyright, he had to reduce his work to a writing. A musician likewise had to produce sheet music or a recording, and a graphic artist either the work itself or a model from which it could be produced. The copyright law does not protect a mere idea which has not been reduced to some tangible form of expression.

The Copyright Law (Title 17, United States Code) lists thirteen classes of copyrightable works, but adds that these "specifications" shall not "limit the subject matter of copyright." Although the law provides that "all writings of an author" are eligible for copyright protection, the courts have indicated that certain types of works (for example, industrial designs and recorded musical performances) which may constitute "writings" in the constitutional sense do not come within the present scope of the copyright law. As a rule of thumb, a work must fit into one of the thirteen categories specified in the statute in order to qualify for statutory protection.

Of particular interest to the artist is *Class G and Class H* of the Copyright Law. *Class G* includes works of the fine arts and works of artistic craftsmanship, insofar as their form but not their mechanical or utilitarian aspects are concerned. Paintings, drawings, sculpture, and the like are included in this category. *Class H* generally covers reproductions of existing works of art in the same or different media. Productions of paintings, sculpture, or other works

15

of art in the form of etchings, drawings, and lithographs are included in this class.

COPYRIGHT OR PATENT: Since confusion may develop over whether a work is subject to a copyright or a patent, it may be advisable to differentiate between the two forms of protection. A *copyright* protects intellectual creations in the form of literary, dramatic, musical, or artistic works, while a *patent* protects inventions in the form of mechanical devices, processes, and the like. A copyright would protect the design of a piece of jewelry, but it would not protect the clasp. It has been held that a statuette mass-produced as a lamp base can be copyrighted. Neither the fact that the figure was associated with a utilitarian object or that it was mass-produced removed this object from the copyrightable category. However, a design for a utilitarian object (for example, a housing for a mixmaster) would be protected under patent rather than copyright laws.

What is protected by a copyright is the manner of expressing an idea, not the idea or subject itself. A copyright precludes anyone from imitating the artist's painting of the Eiffel Tower or a Campbell soup can, but it does not prevent someone else from making his own painting of the same subject matter, even from the same point of view. In other words, it is intentional copying, not accidental duplication, that is prohibited. Consequently, no one checks before issuing copyright papers to determine whether or not the applicant appears to have duplicated the subject of some earlier work; patent is given only after the Patent Office has searched the records of existing patents and concluded that the invention is both novel and utilitarian.

Who Can Secure A Copyright.

If an object is copyrightable, the question then arises who can secure and hold a copyright? As previously discussed, the rights bestowed by copyright legislation merely replace and legally secure those post-publication rights the creator enjoyed under the common law. The post-publicaton rights were actually an extension of the common law pre-publication rights, which are still in existence.

According to the common law, the right to control the reproduction of unpublished works belonged exclusively to the creator. It is only when an artist does work for another, either as an employee or by accepting a commission, that the common law, pre-publication copyright belongs to another and may be converted without the consent of the creator into a statutory, post-publication copyright. Therefore, where a work can be shown to have been made for hire, the employer is given all property rights in the very first instance, whether or not he had anything to do with the creation of the work, and the creator's rights are limited to those which may be specified in his employment contract.

It is generally accepted that the copyright follows the work of art even where the art work was created without a specific purchaser in mind. This may be varied by contractual agreement. The artist can agree to transfer a picture to his client, while reserving for himself all rights to reproduce the picture (see Appendix V for a sample agreement reserving a copyright). In this case, the client receives a tangible object, the painting, stripped of all reproduction rights. Any agreement of this type should include a provision allowing the artist to gain reasonable access to the art work, so that he can reproduce it.

A copyright is considered a transferable piece of property which may accompany, or be separated from the original work from which it came into being. A copyright is also regarded as a divisible piece of property, which may be transferred in whole or in part. The holder of a copyright may license a printer to publish in a certain country or in a specified medium, while reserving for himself the right to publish in other localities or in other forms. Likewise, when the owner of a copyright dies, the property right devolves in accordance with the testator's will, or by the laws of succession when there is no will.

If there is no written agreement to the contrary, the

sale of a work of art, prior to publication, carries with it the common law copyright. The artist should be aware of this when he sells his work. If, on the other hand, the work has been published (made so widely public that a court would consider it a part of the public domain), the common law copyright will have been destroyed and the purchaser will only receive a tangible art work without any copyright privileges. In this situation, the purchaser cannot perfect a statutory copyright since the common law copyright would not pass with the sale of the object.

Legal Protection Offered By Copyright.

If a work of art is reproduced in violation of a statutory copyright, the copyright holder has recourse to a number of different legal remedies. Each of the following may be requested individually or cumulatively: (1) injunctive relief; (2) either the actual damages suffered by the copyright owner together with profits made by the infringer, or statutory damages; and (3) the right to have the infringing material impounded by the court. As a final measure of relief, the court may, in its discretion, compel the infringer to pay court costs and reasonable attorney's fees expended by the owner of the copyright.

The remedies discussed above are those available when an infringement of a statutory copyright has occurred. When a common law (pre-publication) copyright is infringed, the remedies would be those provided by the laws of each individual state. The remedies available under state law would be much the same as those for infringement of the federal statutory copyright, except that the rules for determining the measure of damages would be inapplicable and the remedy which permits the destruction of plates or copies, might not be available.

What Constitutes An Infringement.

It should be evident from our previous discussion that to be an "infringement" there must be an actual copying or reproducing of a copy. A photographer's right in his copyrighted picture is not infringed if another person photographs the same subject. And where the question at issue concerns a copyrighted reproduction of an art work already in the public domain, the slightest difference between original and subsequent reproductions is likely to be sufficient to absolve the second publisher from a charge of copying the reproduction. On the other hand, were a person to discover and prepare a catalogue of the unpublished works of an artist, it is likely that he would be found in violation of the common law copyright. It would be presumed, were an effort to catalogue undertaken, that it was economically advantageous to the publisher, and that the artist's works were being unlawfully appropriated without just compensation.

An infringement may, therefore, be a use of the whole work or a use of some distinguishable part of the whole (if that small part of the work would normally be included in a catalogue by itself). However, one may infringe by copying the bulk of a work with only such minor differences as might be included to avoid the appearance of having copied. An infringement in the field of visual arts would undoubtedly become a close question of fact. There has been little or no litigation in this area.

The courts do not want to foreclose a popular theme (soup cans, for instance) by granting to the first person who paints the subject a right to prohibit anyone else from doing so. On the other hand, the courts cannot allow the inept copyist to escape the penalties for infringement by virtue of his inability to copy exactly, or the plagiarist to escape by creating small intentional differences. Courts must examine the facts in each case to decide if an infringement has occurred.

The question of infringement may arise in the context of a parody. A parody is a humorous imitation of a serious artistic creation, and to be a recognizable parody, the imitator must rely on certain elements of the original work, which are recognized as such. It has been held, over much criticism, that a parody by Jack Benny of a movie took so many elements of the original as to become an infringement. The defense, of course, claimed that Jack Benny, a recognized humorist, should have a right to comment upon the artistic works of another. Nevertheless, in view of this decision, the courts are likely to find an infringement in situations where the borrowing is very extensive and liberal, and where the parody is undertaken primarily with a view toward profit rather than toward meaningful criticism.

FAIR USE: This raises the question of the "fair use" doctrine. This concept is not even mentioned in the Copyright Statute, but has been established by the courts in an effort to avoid the unfairness that might result if the copyright owner's rights were considered absolutely exclusive. The courts have held that if the user has a valid reason to use a small portion of the copyrighted work, and if the use does not adversely affect the owner's interest, it will be treated as a "fair use" and not an infringement. It is clear that a brief quote from a book in a book review would not be an infringement. Presumably, too, the reproduction by a newspaper of a prize winner in an art competition would be a fair use, as would the publication of a picture of an art work in conjunction with a critical article. Whether reproductions in an art history, or in a biography of a painter would constitute a fair use becomes more questionable in view of a judicial decision holding that a mere cataloguing of art works is a violation of the copyright.

When quoting, copying or reproducing it is advisable to seek permission of the copyright holder. The Copyright Office can be helpful in tracing a copyright owner, and the Reference Division, Copyright Office, Library of Congress, Washington, D. C. will undertake a search of its records for a nominal fee. If there is any question of the applicability of the fair use doctrine for a projected use, it would be advisable to consult an attorney.

The fair use doctrine is not applicable to articles that are not under copyright, either because the article has

20

been dedicated to the public, the copyright has expired, or the article was not subject to a statutory copyright in the first place. A copyright may be obtained on a new version of an article already in the public domain; for example, on a reproduction of an original painting or on a revised edition of a book. The new copyright covers only the characteristics of the new version that distinguish it from the original. In fact, it is not possible to obtain any exclusive rights in the property itself when it is not protected by a copyright. For example, the annotations, introduction, and art reproductions in an edition of the Notebooks of Leonardo da Vinci, and possibly the translation as well, may be subject to copyright protection, but the Notebooks themselves are available for reprinting in an edition that does not use any of the copyrightable parts of the present edition.

There is no fair use exception for articles under common law copyright—articles that have not yet been published. A work which is not yet published is not a subject of concern to the world; it is not news, neither does the public need responsible commentary, for the work itself is not available to the public.

NON-COPYRIGHTABLE WORKS: Some classes of objects are not copyrightable at all, consequently their reproduction cannot constitute a copyright infringement. These include devices for measuring or computing, such as rulers or slide rules, charts of heights and weights, calendars (though artistic reproductions associated with them may be), tables or lists that are taken from public documents and involve no creative work, formulas or systems and devices based on them, etc. Some of these classes of items may, however, be patentable.

The rule against copyrighting immoral or libelous works is a curious one. It does not prevent the author from making an effort to obtain a copyright since the Copyright Office does not examine the merits of the submitted works. Whether a work is libelous or immoral is within the domain of a court upon application by the copyright holder for an order to enjoin for an infringement. The alleged infringer can defend by charging that the work is immoral and therefore never really had an effective copyright. Presumably, a court would apply tests used in other contexts in arriving at a decision that a work of art is libelous or obscene.

How to Secure a Copyright.

The essence of a copyright is the giving of public notice that, though an object is exposed to the public, the artist or owner of the copyright is not dedicating the work of art to the public domain. The copyright law merely provides the means for giving such notice, and if the statutory procedures are followed, the copyright owner will not surrender his rights. It is important to remember that while the Copyright Office registers claims to copyright, it does not grant a copyright.

Certain types of art work are eligible for copyright registration before they have even been published. These include works of art, musical compositions, dramas, drawings and plastic works of a scientific or technical character, photographs, motion pictures, and works prepared for oral delivery. The following types of material *cannot* be registered for copyright as unpublished works: books, prints, maps, commercial prints and labels, and reproductions of works of art. The advantages in registering works for copyright prior to publication is that the types of relief provided in the federal copyright laws may be sought if there is an unlawful infringement.

If an *unpublished* work qualifies for a statutory copyright, the applicant must register a claim in the Copyright Office. This is done by writing to the Register of Copyrights, Library of Congress, Washington, D. C., and requesting the proper application form for the type of work to be copyrighted. The applicant must then mail to the Register a photograph or other identifying reproduction of the work, an application form and a fee of $4.00. No copyright notice is required for unpublished works. If the work is later reproduced in copies and published, the law requires that a second registration be made and that all copies of the published form contain the statutory copyright notice. This procedure and the form of copyright notice to be used is the same as that followed for a published work and is outlined below.

In the case of a work that has been *published*, it is essential that all copies distributed in the United States contain the statutory copyright notice. The statutory copyright notice may consist of (1) the word "Copyright," the abbreviation "Copr.," or the symbol "©," (2) the name of the claimant, and (3) the year of first publication (although this is normally not required); for example:

"Copyright" (or *"Copr."* or *"©"*) *Fred Roe* 1962.

In order not to deface certain graphic works, an alternative notice is available. It consists of the symbol "©" accompanied by the initials, monogram or mark of the copyright owner, but the owner's name must appear on some accessible part of the work. If the symbol "©" is used the copyright may gain international protection as well (see discussion of International Copyright at pages 29 to 30). The problem of providing adequate notice can, at times, be difficult. For example, what if the art work is a repetitive design on wallpaper or cloth? Is it appropriate to place the copyright symbol or mark on the selvage of wallpaper, which may be covered up once the wallpaper is applied? Aside from a few unusual situations which may be encountered, the mere giving of notice in the statutory form on all copies is sufficient as a first step in securing a statutory copyright.

After affixing proper notice to the object, the second step is to deposit "promptly" with the Register of Copyrights two complete copies of "the best edition then published" along with a registration form and the statutory fee of $4.00. Where the work to be copyrighted has not been reproduced but is an original plastic or graphic work, one photograph may be submitted in lieu of the two copies. If the work is later reproduced, two copies of the reproduction must be submitted. Upon proper registration, the Register of Copyrights will issue a certificate which will serve as prima facie evidence of all the facts stated thereon. Should the claimant fail to submit copies after publication, and after a demand from the Register, a fine may be levied and copyright protection will be lost. However, the mere failure to submit a copy or copies to the Register will not preclude the copyright holder from initiating a lawsuit for infringement if, before suing, he submits the required copies.

The law provides two consecutive copyright terms, each running for 28 years. The initial copyright period runs from the time of publication, not registration. A work published in 1958, but not registered until 1959, would be copyrighted as of 1958. To be entitled to the 28 years extension, a work published in 1958 would have to be re-registered sometime during the year 1985. When a reproduction is made at a date subsequent to the filing of the original, the copyright year on the reproduction will be the date of the original filing, not the date of the publication of the reproduction.

It is advisable to consult an attorney if one is interested in copyrighting different versions of the same work. Improperly done, such a copyright may be ineffective and result in the loss of rights in either the original, the new version, or both.

When Is A Work Published.

As previously mentioned, certain works are eligible for copyright only upon proper publication with notice of copyright attached. These works should be distinguished from those that may be registered in their unpublished form, but which must be re-registered at the time of publication. In either case, the artist should be aware of those acts that may constitute publication.

The reader must remember that publication operates in two ways; publication with notice is sufficient to create a statutory copyright (presuming the work is subsequently registered without difficulty), while publication without notice will result in a public dedication of the work. But how much exposure and what type of public display is sufficient to effect a statutory copyright or, on the other hand, to erase a common law copyright? Would the same degree of public exhibition that is necessary to perfect a statutory copyright be sufficient to destroy a common law copyright? The answer apparently is no! The law seems to be that a minimal showing to the public is necessary to effect a statutory copyright, while a fairly wide showing is necessary to eliminate the common law copyright. In other words, the law looks favorably on the maintenance of these rights by making it easier to create than to destroy them.

In a well known case, the meaning of publication for purposes of a public dedication of a work of art was at issue. A painter had placed his picture on display in a gallery exhibition. Visitors paid to be admitted and, while no copyright privilege was claimed, the visitors were asked not to reproduce any of the pictures in the show. The court held that this display was not a sufficient publication to destroy the artist's common law copyright. It should be clear, however, that if notice of a copyright had been placed on the picture, the exhibition would have been a sufficient publication to perfect a statutory copyright.

As a general rule, if it is apparent that a distribution or exhibition is for a specific and limited purpose, the common law copyright will not be affected. For instance, if an artist circulates his work among friends and critics for criticism, this should not result in the loss of the common law copyright. If, on the other hand, the work is displayed so as to reasonably lead others to believe that the work is dedicated to the public, it will be so treated, regardless of the artist's true motives.

Transfer Of A Copyright.

The copyright statute distinguishes between ownership of the copyright and the ownership of the material object which has been copyrighted. The statute further provides that the mere transfer of the material object "shall not of itself constitute a transfer of the copyright." A copyright may be assigned, granted, mortgaged, or bequeathed by will.

Since the law recognizes a difference between giving a copyright, which is termed an assignment, and merely permitting someone to use the copyright, which is known as a license, the act of transferring a copyright may have important legal consequences. For example, there may be substantially different tax consequences if a work of art is assigned, rather than licensed. Moreover, whether a particular transfer is deemed as an assignment or license may also be important in deciding whether a reputed owner has the proper standing to bring a lawsuit in his own name for infringement. If the transaction takes the form of a license, the licensee must join the copyright holder in the lawsuit; when the copyright owner and the licensee are in different states there may be problems concerning the court of proper jurisdiction.

The recording section of the copyright law refers only to "assignments," and unfortunately the dividing line between assignments and other instruments, such as exclusive licenses, mortgages and discharges, is far from being clear. (See Appendix VII for a sample assignment of copyright). Hence, it is a wise precaution to record in the Copyright Office instruments by which the ownership of exclusive rights is transferred and in the event of litigation to leave it to a court of law to decide what type of transaction was actually involved. Unless the assignment is recorded within three months after its execution (or within six months if the transfer occurs outside the United States), the statute provides that it is "void as against any subsequent purchaser or mortgagee for a valuable consideration, without notice, whose assignment has been duly recorded." Even if the three or six month period has elapsed (as the case may be) there is still considerable value in recording an assignment since recordation is required, in any case, before the name of the new owner may be substituted in the new notice of copyright.

There is no special form for registering a transfer of interest in a copyright. Either the document itself or a notarized copy should be sent to the Register of Copyrights. (If the transfer takes place outside the United States, the transferor must acknowledge the document before a consular or legation officer who is empowered to administer oaths and act as a notary.) The Register of Copyrights will photo-duplicate the document and return it to the copyright holder. The fee for registering a transfer is three dollars if the document is less than six pages in length and in respect to books, if it covers no more than one title. If the document is longer, or more than one title of a book is involved, there is an additional charge of fifty cents per page or per extra title. The appropriate sum should accompany the document when mailed to the Register.

Protection Of Titles.

The artist cannot copyright the title of his work, only the work of art, itself. However, a court may protect the title under certain circumstances by applying the theory of unfair competition. The theory behind guarding against unfair competition is that the user should not be permitted to capitalize on the efforts of another and to deceive the public. In those cases where a title has acquired an "everyday" meaning, courts will be sympathetic to the original user. Generally the courts apply the following tests to determine if the title has acquired an "everyday" meaning: (1) the extent of its advertising and popularization; (2) the period of time that the title has been used, and (3) the public reaction over a period of time to the title. It should be emphasized that the mere adoption of a title does not give it protection, but once the title has gained an "everyday" meaning it may be protected (if there is a likelihood of deception or confusion) against even innocent usage by another. (The theory of Unfair Competition is discussed in greater detail at pages 37 to 38).

The Moral Right Doctrine.

The moral right doctrine is of European origin and has only limited application in the United States. This doctrine reserves a bundle of "paternity rights" to the artist even though the artist may have disposed of his copyright. Among these moral rights is the right to preserve the integrity of the work against alteration, the right to maintain authorship of a work, the right to deny attribution if the author so chooses, and the right to deny exhibition without proper creditation.

In the United States, an artist has no right to prevent the alteration of his work unless he specifically contracts for that right when he sells his work. A novelist, for instance, would want to include in a contract to sell his book to a movie producer a clause permitting him to veto any adaptation that was not consistent in spirit with the original. Likewise, an artist might wish to insert a similar clause in a contract with a company which proposes to make and market reproductions of one of his paintings. If the artist takes this precaution, he should be protected against the embarrassment which may result if something is published over his name that is unfaithful and damaging to the original.

The rights best described as "paternity rights" may be guarded by state law in the absence of national copyright law protection. Protection under state law may be realized by applying the theory that it is unfair competition for a person to claim authorship of the work of another, or for a person to attribute to an author works of inferior quality. In addition to applying the doctrine of unfair competition, the violation of paternity rights might be resisted as an invasion of privacy, an actionable libel, or a breach of

28

an implied contract. Where an artist feels that he has been injured by the violation of his paternity rights, he is best advised to counsel with an attorney.

International Copyright.

In 1954, the United States ratified a major multilateral agreement covering the subject of international copyright. This agreement, known as the Universal Copyright Convention, brought the United States into a partnership which protects works of art copyrighted in member nations. Prior to the Universal Copyright Convention, reciprocal recognition of copyrights depended either on bilateral agreements between individual nations, or upon the covenants of the Berne Convention to which the United States was not a party.

The Universal Copyright Convention, of which the United States is a member, requires a contracting nation to accord works by nationals of other countries party to the Convention the same degree of protection as it accords works of its own nationals. Compliance with the formalities of acquiring copyright in the various member states is excused if the notice prescribed by the Convention is followed. This notices consists of "©," the year, and the name of the proprietor of the copyright. In essence, therefore, all "foreign" published works covered by the Convention are protected automatically in contracting nations by publication with the prescribed notice.

The copyright owner should remember that under the United States Copyright Code, the notice of copyright may include either the word "Copyright," the abbreviation "Copr.," or the symbol "©." The use of the word or abbreviation in place of the symbol does not satisfy the requirements of the Universal Copyright Convention. Failure to use the legend prescribed by the Convention may protect the copyright in the United States, but will not secure reciprocal protection in member nations.

In some instances, nations have become a party to more than one Convention. The Buenos Aires Convention, for example, represents the only other attempt the United States has taken toward international copyright protection on a multilateral basis. To date, some eighteen Western Hemisphere countries have ratified the Buenos Aires Convention, which recites that the law of the member country where the work originated determines what formalities must be followed initially to perfect a copyright. The words "Copyright Reserved," "All Rights Reserved," "Directos Reservados," or the equivalent would most likely meet the requirements of this Convention.

In order to gain an effective copyright in a foreign country the provisions of the applicable treaties must be examined. Where a nation is not a party to a multilateral treaty, it may be advisable to have the work of art published in that country so as to become eligible for local copyright protection. It is recommended that a lawyer be consulted before a work of art is published in a foreign country.

Conclusion.

We have discussed the nature of copyrights, outlined those steps in securing a copyright that can be safely performed by the claimant, and suggested the kinds of problems that might arise which best require the services of a lawyer. It would be wrong to conclude, however, without mentioning once again that the Copyright Office itself is most gracious and helpful in supplying information to those with specific copyright problems. The artist should not hesitate to write the Office when he has a copyright problem.

Chapter 3

INVASION OF PRIVACY, LIBEL, DISPARAGEMENT, UNFAIR COMPETITION, AND IMITATION

Art is a mode of visual perception and reflects the way the artist sees the world about him. The naive person insists that there is only one way to see the world—the way that it appears to his own immediate vision. This is not true, since we see what we learn to see, and our vision becomes by habit a careful selection of all that there is to see. And what we want to see is determined by our desire to discover or construct a meaningful world. Art in that way becomes a construction of the artist's reality.

In constructing his version of reality, the artist must be concerned with a series of legal wrongs that he may commit in the creative process, or that may be perpetrated upon him in the practice of his profession. The law which permeates the artist's environment, serves to protect an individual from suffering either personal or economic injury. Protection is accorded by permitting recourse to the courts in the following circumstances: (1) where the details of a person's life, his name, his reputation, or a pictorial representation of him are appropriated without obtaining proper consent, there is an *invasion of privacy*; (2) where the property of an individual is unlawfully appropriated for economic gain, it is *unfair competition*; (3) where an untrue statement damages a person's reputation or standing in the community, it is *libel* (written state-

31

ment) or *slander* (verbal statement); and (4) where an untrue statement damages a product or property, it is *disparagement*. At times, it is difficult to distinguish between wrongs. "John Doe makes a lousy violin," might be interpreted as libel against John Doe, disparagement of his violin, or both. These wrongs and their legal consequences are the subject matter of this chapter.

Invasion of Privacy.

The concept that it is a tort, or personal injury, to expose the name, picture or details of the life of a private citizen is based on the belief that there is an innate right to be left alone — a so-called right of privacy. Invasion of privacy, as an actionable common law tort, came into being in the late 1890's on the theory that, in an increasingly complex society, with a press demanding more and more material for publication, it was necessary to protect a person's right simply to be left alone. Because of its relatively recent development, the law respecting the right of privacy has not developed to the same extent as the law respecting long established torts. Consequently, there is confusion about even quite fundamental issues in this field of the law.

Generally, a person who is not newsworthy has the most compelling argument in favor of protecting a right of privacy. However, even those who have become newsworthy may object to an unsolicited invasion of their private lives when exposure is unrelated to their public image or activities. While it is appropriate to discuss or comment on those aspects of a politician's life that affect his suitability for public office, the details of his family life are generally private, unless he chooses to make them public (as politicians with large and attractive families are wont to do). A person, then, may voluntarily place in the public domain aspects of his life that could not otherwise properly be the subject of comment and criticism.

There are circumstances, however, where the private life of a person is sufficiently interesting to the public that publication without actual or implied consent is permissible. Of course, this statement assumes that the publication is not defamatory or too intimate. A leading case in this area concerned *The New Yorker* magazine profile of a child prodigy who had in his mature years retreated into obscurity. The fact that this person had once been newsworthy and that the public had a reasonable interest in what had happened to him were considered adequate justifications for publishing a report of his present day circumstance.

The artist is most likely to commit the tort of invasion of privacy by producing and showing a representation of a person without permission. The point has already been made that an artist whose portrait of a subject was rejected might commit an invasion of privacy by showing it or disposing of it to a third person. Obviously, the details of a person's private life may be exposed graphically, rather than in words. Obviously, too, a visual work depicting someone who is well known may have increased value. If produced without permission of the subject, such a work may fall in that hazy area where invasion of privacy and unfair competition meet. One way for the artist to guard against a lawsuit for an invasion of privacy is to ask for written releases from all parties concerned. Care should be exercised when a minor is involved, since releases from minors are void and must be executed by the parent or the guardian. The release should include the purpose to which the released material is to be put. A model release is reproduced in Appendix VIII.

The artist may, of course, be subjected to invasions of his own privacy. He has a right to protect himself from reports of his personal life (though not from comments on his work). Moreover, the artist may resort to a court of law to enjoin others from profiting from the use of his name or his likeness.

The vast majority of cases involving an invasion of privacy occur where there has been a fairly wide publication or distribution of the material constituting the invasion. Mere word of mouth comments (unless uttered on radio or television) probably will not support an action for invasion of privacy, although this issue is still largely unresolved. On the other hand, the amount of publication necessary to support a case for libel or slander has been more thoroughly litigated over the years, and in those cases the most minimal publication will generally support a case.

Libel.

Any defamatory material which tends to degrade a man in the eyes of his neighbor or to injure his property or business may be considered libelous and give rise to a cause of action for damages suffered. Since libelous material may be published by a writing, an effigy, or a picture, it is therefore advisable for the artist to consider carefully the subject matter of his work before it is published or exhibited.

In most states, no specific injury to the plaintiff needs to be shown in order to collect damages; the injury is presumed from the publication and the character of the statement. The actual damage in a libel case is not harm to the feelings of the person libeled, but the effect on his reputation in society. A person has a right to protect the public image he wishes to display, and it is no defense to a libel charge to argue that most people would not consider the statement defamatory. In a sense, then, libel is the very opposite of invasion of privacy. In an invasion of privacy, the right protected is to have people unaware of one's life; it might be called the right to withdraw, whereas the right to be free from libel is a protection of one's public image.

At times, it is difficult to determine whether certain material will be held libelous. Statements or graphic portrayals may not outwardly appear to libel anyone, or they may accidently libel a person with whom they are not actually concerned. In the first category are statements that do not make direct reference to a specific person, but instead refer to and identify that person by a set of circumstances that would be familiar to some people. In the second category are cases of unintended reference—where, for example, one man is described and something is said of him which, if untrue, would be libelous, and then another man appears who fits this description or who carries the same name. An example of an unintended reference occurred when a newspaper printed a photograph of a man and woman with a caption indicating an intended marriage. In fact, this man was already married. His wife promptly sued the newspaper and received a judgment on grounds that friends and acquaintances inferred that she was not the wife but, instead, the mistress of the man pictured in the newspaper. In this case, the libellant (newspaper) did not even refer to the plaintiff—the wife—and the statement itself was not libelous, but only damaging when taken in conjunction with the fact, of which the libellant had no knowledge, that the man was already married. In a few states, it is required that where a libel is not clear and complete in itself, the plaintiff has the burden of proving special injury in order to receive a judgment. In these states the inference that there must have been injury is abandoned.

A libel must also be published, which means simply that it must be read by some third party. Therefore, it is not liberous to send an insulting letter to a person, but if the letter is sent by messenger in an unsealed envelope and he reads it, or if it is sent by post card so that post office employees can read it, libel may be found. However, if the recipient permits a private, defamatory letter to be read, the sender is not guilty of publishing. On the other hand, where the sender knows the recipient to be blind or illiterate, so that the letter will have to be read to him, the sender is guilty of publishing a libel.

In a charge of libel, the defendant may respond with the defense that the publication was truthful. However, the burden of proving the truth of the statement is on the defendant. The defendant cannot merely say that he believed the statement true, or that it was told him on good authority, or that the plaintiff has the reputation of doing what was reported. The defendant must actually prove that his statement is essentially true, although some variance in detail is permitted. By placing the burden of proving truthfulness upon the defendant, libel suits become rather difficult to defend. And where the libel charged alleges the commission of a crime, the defendant asserting the truth of his statement may even have to prove it beyond a reasonable doubt; that is, according to the standard of proof that would be used in a criminal court, rather than the civil standard, which is preponderance of the evidence.

Besides asserting that a statement alleged to be libelous is true, a defendant in a libel suit may raise other affirmative defenses. If the plaintiff consents to the libel by publishing the statement himself, or the communication is privileged, the defendant may properly defend his case. Privileged communications include the transmittal of information, damaging or not, where the recipient, an employer or lender for instance, has a legitimate interest in knowing the type of information communicated, or where the sender is attempting to protect his interests or those of one near to him. In the public sphere, one may repeat a statement found in public records and not be guilty of libel, though the statement be false. There will be, of course, a difference of opinion of how public a record must be to qualify in support of this defense.

Another defense to a lawsuit for libel is the right to offer fair comment. For the artist, fair comment is a two-edged sword. The artist may justly comment upon, or even ridicule in words or in graphic art, the works of others. He is, of course, subject to the same sort of comment and criticism from others. Every man who publishes commits himself to the judgment of the public.

It should be evident throughout this discussion that there is no requirement of intent before finding a person guilty of libel. One can libel quite accidentally. Whether a libel is innocent or malicious will be taken into consideration in assessing damages, but not in determining whether a libel has been committed.

Disparagement.

Disparagement is a form of defamation that reduces or even destroys the value or marketability of property. As in a case of libel, disparagement must be published to a third party, it must be untruthful, and it must refer to the plaintiff. It may, however, be written or spoken and, unlike a libel action, injury is not presumed but must be proven. Just because the artist is unable to sell his work as a result of a disparaging remark, the person who uttered the statement is not necessarily at fault and liability must be demonstrated.

It has been held that a statement charging that a gallery represented a copy to be the original was disparaging where the picture was the original. It has also been held, surprisingly enough, that a publisher had an action for disparagement when it was said of one of its textbooks that it was a laughingstock among intelligent teachers. I use the word "surprisingly" for it would seem that this statement would come within the range of fair comment on literary and artistic matters. And even where it is shown that the artist or author has been unable to sell his products as a result of a disparaging remark that would be called a fair comment, the person who uttered the remark is not liable.

It is also not defamatory to "puff" one's own products, even where there is an implied criticism of another's. A man may generally say, "I produce the best baby-food," or that "oil is safer than gas for heating." If the artist makes a statement to the effect that his work is superior to that of another artist, it may be protected under the recognized privilege to "puff" and also as a fair comment on the work of another. In criticizing the work of another the artist must recognize that there is a fine distinction between fair comment and disparagement.

Unfair Competition.

Where an artist's work has gained a certain value, it is a form of unfair competition for another party to reap that value without consent. This legal theory was discussed in the chapter on Copyrights, but it is worth repeating that this tort encompasses the wrongful appropriation of an intangible.

Under certain circumstances the prohibition on unfair competition will protect the title of a work of art even though a title is not subject to copyright. This is especially true where a novel has been very successful and a movie producer uses the title to cash in on the reputation of the novel. The title of a painter's work, however, may be subject to wrongful appropriation and exploitation if it is as famous as the "MONA LISA" or "A SUNDAY AFTERNOON ON THE ISLAND OF LA GRANDE JATTE."

In many respects, the law of unfair competition resembles the law against invasion of privacy. The latter guards against the appropriation of intangibles that are intentionally kept out of the market place. The former protects against the appropriation of those intangibles that are intended to be commercially exploited. In either case, something of value has been taken from the creator.

Imitation In Art.

Lawsuits for plagiarism are more prevalent in works of fiction, drama and music, than in the graphic arts. Undoubtedly, this paucity of litigation over purported imitation in the graphic arts is a direct result of the artist's understanding that a given period will produce many works of art similar in style and theme. Mature artists understand that art is a combination of personal physical and mental experiences which are often influenced by the style of other masters. The work of such masters carries an impact that results in waves of influence on younger or less experienced artists. These recognized artists need not necessarily be indignant when they find many of their ideas are used by other artists. Sometimes this is a source of gratification.

In any event, a reticence to press litigation for plagiarism is probably a good thing. It is not desirable that the intellectual and artistic treasures of a society be too stringently restricted by personal monopolies. In a sense, the person who creates a work of art after seeing another, has contributed something of value to society. Frequently, this artist will refine prior techniques or even stimulate greater public enthusiasm for the subject matter. Most likely, this artist's creation will not materially affect the ability of the first artist to dispose of his work, and may even give the work of the first artist greater value and public acceptance.

The right or freedom to imitate does not permit an individual to copy or wrongfully appropriate the creations of another artist. The creator has every right to enjoy the economic fruits of his labors. But, as our copyright law clearly recognizes, the artist should not be entitled to gain a monopoly of a theme, a subject, or an idea.

Conclusion.

The legal remedies discussed in this chapter by no means exhaust the avenues of protection available to the artist. These theories of law should be a starting point, however, for the artist to determine whether any of his vested legal rights have been violated. If redress is planned, the artist should seek the advice of a competent attorney.

Chapter 4

THE ARTIST AND INCOME TAXES

Hopefully, the artist will receive income from his work. This means that he is likely to have to pay taxes. But, as every citizen, the artist has the right to take advantage of all of the provisions of the Internal Revenue Code that can save him tax money. He must also play by the rules and pay what is due. Several provisions of the Internal Revenue Code are especially relevant to the artist. It is the purpose of this chapter to examine some of these provisions, rather than the income tax structure as a whole. The assumption is that the reader is familiar in a general way with those provisions with which the ordinary taxpayer is likely to come in contact. Our discussion is intended primarily to acquaint the artist with those sections which may apply to him — not a complete income tax guide.

Averaging Income — "Spreading Back"

A man who earns a steady income of $10,000 per year will pay less income tax in a five year period than the man who earns $6,000 for four years and $26,000 in the fifth year. Yet both have earned a total of $50,000. This doesn't seem equitable, especially when the extraordinary income in the fifth year is the final payment on a project that has required five years to complete. It was this inequity that prompted Congress to include an averaging or spreading provision in the Internal Revenue Code. This provision allows the taxpayer to treat some of the extraordinary income as if it has been earned in equal parts over a five year period.

Assume that an artist has been earning $6,000 a year and

suddenly is paid $26,000 for two or three big commissions in the fifth year. If the artist were to pay his taxes the fifth year on the ordinary basis, he would pay a tax of $9,-600. What happens to the artist's tax if he takes advantage of the averaging provision?

First of all, the government does not want to create a complicated tax calculation if there is only a slight variation in income received over a period of years. The income that can be averaged, or treated as if it were earned over a five year period, is only that which exceeds by more than one-third the average income for the preceding four years. It is assumed that a fluctuation of one-third is not sufficiently abnormal to require income spreading. In the fact situation described above the averageable income in the year $26,000 was earned would be $18,000. That is because the average income of the preceding four years was $6,000; the one-third normal fluctuation was $2,000; the averageable income was the income in excess of $8,000 (average + 1/3); and $26,000 — $8,000 = $18,000. If the averageable income turns out to be $3,000 or less, averaging is not to be permitted, presumably because the saving is not worth the trouble.

The $18,000 averageable income is treated as if it were earned in equal portions of $3,600 per year over the five year averaging period. Because you pay a different tax rate depending upon the amount of income earned in any given year, the government had to decide in what bracket this extra $3,600 per year should be treated as falling. It could have said, recalculate your tax for each of the preceding four years as if you had earned an extra $3,600 in each of those years, add up the taxes you owe, and pay that. The system which evolved looks a little complicated, but it is easier than recomputing taxes for the last four years. Another big "as if" is thrown in, but once the nature of that "as if" is understood, the system can be seen to be relatively simple. The assumption made is that a tax had been paid in each of the preceding four years on 4/3rd the average income of those four years—in other words we are back to the old $8,000 figure. The $3,600 averageable income is now added to the assumed $8,000 income, giving a hypothetical averaged income of $11,600. The tax to be paid for each year is the difference between the tax on $11,600 and the tax, assumed to have been paid, on the $8,000. In other words, the tax to be paid on the $3,600 is calculated as if it were on the last $3,600 of income of a person earning $11,600. And, in general terms, the averageable income assigned to each year of the averaging period is taxed at a rate as if it were added to 4/3rds the average income of the preceding four years.

In this case, the tax on the top $3,600 is $1,154 per year. (The tax on $11,600 is $2,904; that on $8,000, which is assumed to have been paid, is $1,750; the tax due is therefore $1,154.) The tax on the total averageable income of $18,000 is five times the tax on the amount assigned to each year, or $5,770.

The unaverageable income for the fifth year is $8,000. That is taxed at the ordinary rate. The tax, we already know, would be $1,750. The total tax on $26,000 averaged over five years, then, would be $7,520—$5,770 on the averageable portion and $1,750 on the unaverageable portion. The normal tax on an income of $26,000 in one year would have been $9,600. Averaging, complicated as it may seem, turned out to be a very easy way of saving $2,080.

The averaging provisions may be used for most forms of income. Prior to 1964, however, the taxpayer had to demonstrate that the income was derived from projects that had been in process during the period for which the averaging was to be allowed. Under the 1964 revision, even extraordinary income obtained in a few moments, from a TV quiz show, for example, may be averaged. The award in a law suit involving breach of contract can also be averaged. In brief, any extraordinary income is averageable, except income from capital gains (the profit from selling capital investments, such as stocks, a studio, or depreciable equipment), gambling winnings, gifts or bequests, and some premature distributions under pension plans.

"SPREADING FORWARD": An artist may well receive part of his income in royalties from sales, for example, of a copyrighted print or reproduction, a book that the artist illustrated, or a commercial product the artist designed. Royalty receipts to the creator are also treated as ordinary income, rather than as capital gains.

Royalty receipts, like commissions, tend to bunch up in a single year. Such receipts may be treated under the spreading provisions of the Internal Revenue Code just mentioned, but in some situations the artist may be better off if he arranges with his publisher or licensee to have the income paid over several years, rather than all in one year. Such an arrangement is called "spreading forward" or deferring income. As a general rule, established artists make agreements to actually spread their income forward, while rising artists, whose incomes have been going up are more likely to be benefited by the "spreading back" provisions of the Code.

An artist who expects to receive something like $50,000 in royalties can enter into an agreement limiting the royalty payments to $10,000 in any one year, regardless of the fact that more royalties have accrued to his account. This spreading forward of income is permissible as long as the artist reports his income as it is received, and not on an accrual basis. The artist must exercise great caution in entering into this type of agreement so as not to gain any control or economic benefit from royalties that have accrued but are not yet paid. If it appears that the artist has gained some control of or benefit from unpaid royalties, the Internal Revenue Service is likely to argue that the royalties have been received and are therefore taxable. Any rights to withdraw the accrued amount, any segregation of funds by the artist's payor, and any power to accelerate the payments must be scrupulously avoided. It is best to rely simply upon the general credit of the company paying the royalty, than to demand any kind of note that might be interpreted an equivalent to the royalties due.

These two methods of spreading out income to reduce

taxes must be considered carefully in each factual situation; what is advantageous for one taxpayer may not be for another. The artist with bunched income problems would be well advised to seek professional help before deciding which solution to adopt.

Donating Art To Charity.

Most sophisticated art collectors realize that under the tax laws they are entitled to claim a deduction for the fair market value of art that is donated to a recognized charity. By the same token, is the artist who creates art entitled to take a charitable deduction for donating one of his own works to a charitable institution?

It is conceded that the strength of the artist's claim to a charitable deduction for donating his own work is a confused area of the law. The problem is that a person cannot take a deduction for the value of services rendered to a charitable organization. For instance, a public relations man cannot say, "My time is worth $20.00 an hour and I have spent 100 hours organizing a fund drive for my church, so I'll deduct $2,000 as a charitable contribution." The attitude of the Internal Revenue Service is that a person should not be permitted to take charitable deductions for value of time spent in making telephone calls, licking stamps, or standing on a street corner with a tin can. Such contributions of time are likely to be leisure activities, not a contribution of time taken from otherwise productive activities.

On the other hand, if a man who manufactures iron pipe, chooses to give some of that pipe to his church for use in the construction of a new building, he can deduct the difference between the market value of the pipe and the costs and expenses incurred in producing the contributed property. In essence, the issue is whether the artist painting a picture resembles the public relations man giving his time, or the manufacturer donating his product.

It has been held in at least one case that an artist may deduct the value of pictures contributed to a charitable

45

institution. We may assume, however, that the outcome of this case might have been different if the artist had been asked to paint a mural. If the artist donates a painting which he has set aside originally for sale, the resemblance to the manufacturer of pipes becomes more apparent. On the other hand, when the artist paints a picture on request, he resembles the public relations man who voluntarily performed a service.

If an artist claims a deduction for the contribution of his art, he is likely to be questioned by the Internal Revenue Service. Therefore, in order to gain a deduction for the value of a charitable donation, it is advisable for the artist to contribute a work of art he has already created, which is part of his ordinary stock in trade, rather than to create a work of art for the sole purpose of making a charitable contribution. This is based on the supposition that an artist cannot take a charitable deduction for the value of his services, but that he can deduct as a charitable contribution the value of the finished work he contributes. Where the artist contributes one of his completed works, the value of his charitable contribution is calculated by subtracting his costs of producing the painting from its market value.

In making a contribution in kind, the valuation placed on a contribution is a likely source of disagreement between the taxpayer and the Internal Revenue Service. If the artist has a record of sales of comparable pieces, establishing value is relatively easy. However, even without the benefit of such records, some deduction may be allowed. Where the artist was able to produce only limited evidence of market value, one court reduced the artist's valuation considerably, but nevertheless allowed a deduction. For purposes of substantiating a deduction for the donation of a work of art, it is recommended that the artist hire at least three independent appraisers. Although such evidence is by no means binding on the Internal Revenue Service, it will no doubt be considered in valuing the deduction.

In common with donations made by any taxpayer, an

46

artist's charitable contributions will not be deductible where they exceed in the tax year either 20% or 30% of his adjusted gross income for that year (the percentage depending upon the type of institution to which the contribution is made). A person planning to contribute over 20% of his adjusted gross income in one year should consult either a lawyer or the Internal Revenue Service to determine whether circumstances permit the deduction of an extra 10% and whether, if the 30% limit is to be exceeded, the deduction can be carried over and applied to offset income received in another year.

Deductibility of Expenses.

An artist seriously engaged in producing art as a livelihood may subtract expenses of producing art from any income received. The mere fact that the artist realizes no profit after expenses are subtracted from receipts does not mean the artist cannot qualify as being in business. However, if art is merely a hobby and the artist only produces an occasional sale, courts have ruled that the expenses of production cannot be deducted in calculating income. Courts reason that in such a case the taxpayer's activities were recreational. If the artist has any doubt on which side of the line he falls, he should consult an attorney.

Assuming that the artist is in business to sell his work, even if it is a side business, there are a number of expenses he can legitimately deduct in calculating his taxable income for the year. In order to report his taxable income, the artist should file Schedule C of Form 1040 with his income tax return. This form may be obtained from the Internal Revenue Service upon request.

In calculating the costs of goods sold on Schedule C, the artist should include the cost of any materials that go into the finished product, the cost of expendable incidentals that do not go directly into the product (for instance, stationery), the wages of hired help (but not wages paid the taxpayer by himself), and other items directly related to producing and selling the product. This last general category would include, for example, the expenses incurred in traveling to the location where the work is to be exhibited for sale. Such travel must be for a genuine business purpose and the expenses claimed cannot include those of one's family.

Other business deductions are allowed besides those directly related to the cost of producing a work of art. These include rent or depreciation of business property. The artist will normally have a studio, often in his own residence. If the studio is separate from his residence, the artist may deduct the whole rental cost, as well as the heat, utilities, and the like. Where the artist uses a part of his residence, he may assign to his studio a pro rata share of the costs of running his household. If he uses one of five rooms, he can deduct as a business expense 1/5th of the rent (or depreciation where the building is owned), utilities, heat, etc. If the business use of a specific item or service is greater than 1/5th, a larger share can be deducted; for instance, where the same phone is used for business and pleasure, it may be that, though only 1/5th of the space in the house is used for business, 1/2 of the phone service is so used. The artist may also discover that if his studio is in his own home, and he moves from one house to another, the Internal Revenue Service will permit him to deduct that portion of his moving expenses that are attributable to his studio.

Where the artist owns property used in his trade or business, and such property has a useful life exceeding one year, he may depreciate this property on one of several scales provided for in the Internal Revenue Code. The choice of methods of depreciation depends upon whether the artist wants to receive the bulk of his deductions as soon as possible, or, whether he prefers to spread them out evenly over a period of years. Probably the biggest problem for the novice record keeper is to determine what is a reasonable life span over which to depreciate a particular article. The Internal Revenue Service produces a pamphlet explaining the concept of depreciation, which includes the appropriate expected useful life of thousands of kinds of articles, from office furniture to buildings, and from heavy machinery to farm animals. If depreciation becomes a problem for the artist, it is best to consult with an accountant or attorney, or an Internal Revenue Service Agent.

In order to take advantage of these deductions, the artist must keep records. Keeping detailed and precise ledger accounts is not necessary, though it is likely to simplify the process of calculating income tax. Where keeping a running account of transactions seems excessive, receipts, cancelled checks, bills of sale, can be traced at the end of the year. In all cases, the artist should save any documents which substantiate a deduction should there be a review or audit by the Internal Revenue Service.

Prizes and Awards.

Artists frequently receive prizes or awards for outstanding accomplishments in their field of interest. Generally, prizes and awards are includible in the artist's gross income, except in the case of scholarship and fellowship awards, or where an award is made for a religious, charitable, scientific, educational, literary, or other civic achievement. For such an award to be tax free the artist must have been selected without any action on his part, and he must not be required to render substantial future services as a condition to receiving the award. However, such an award does not become taxable merely because the artist submits a written application or makes a personal appearance to plead his case.

If an award or prize does not fall within the exceptions listed, it will be fully taxable. If the prize is other than cash, the income is measured by the fair market value of the prize on the day it is received.

Foreign Artists Earning Income In The United States.

The tax levied on the income of an alien depends on the alien's status as resident or non-resident, and on the nature and source of the alien's income. Once we have sorted out the resident aliens from the non-resident aliens, we can proceed to examine the tax rates applicable to each group. A resident alien is an individual present in the United States who is not a mere transient, and who has no definite intention to terminate his stay. By contrast, an individual who comes to the United States for a particular purpose and can accomplish that purpose promptly, is a transient or a non-resident alien. Under current United States Treasury Regulations, all aliens, because of their alienage, are presumed to be non-residents unless they have (1) filed a declaration of intention to become a United States citizen under the naturalization laws; (2) filed a Form 1078, certificate of residence; or (3) performed certain acts which reveal a definite intention to acquire residence in the United States.

A *resident* alien is generally subject to the same income tax liabilities as a United States citizen, including liability for income earned outside the United States; however, to take advantage of the joint return privilege both husband and wife must be residents. If a resident alien pays a tax to a foreign country he is allowed a credit for such taxes on his United States income tax return, if the country of which he is a *citizen* allows a similar credit to Americans. The reciprocity is required from the country of the alien's citizenship even if this is not the country to which he paid taxes for which he is claiming the credit. If the resident alien cannot claim a credit, he can still take a deduction on his United States income tax return for any foreign taxes paid.

Non-resident aliens are classified according to whether or not they are engaged in trade or business in the United States. As a rule, if personal services are performed in the United States at any time during the year, this would qualify the individual as one being engaged in trade or business. One so engaged is taxed on income derived from sources in the United States at the same rate as United States citizens and is allowed essentially the same deductions with respect to that income. Those not engaged in trade or business in the United States are further divided into two classes, depending on whether their total income from sources within the United States is more or less than $21,200. Those earning less than $21,200 pay a flat 30% tax on gross income including taxable capital gains; no allowances for personal exemptions or deductions are permitted. Those individuals in the second category, income exceeding $21,200, are taxed at the regular normal and surtax rates imposed on citizens and residents, except with respect to capital gains.

The non-lawyer should be made aware of the traps that hide in some of this statutory language. For instance, whether income is from sources within the United States may become a complicated question when the income in question is a stock dividend from a corporation doing business both within and without the United States. Whether or not a person is engaged in trade or business may be equally difficult to determine.

United States Citizens Earning Income Abroad.

The situation may also arise where an artist, who is a citizen of the United States, earns income in a foreign country. An American artist may qualify for preferential tax treatment on income earned in a foreign country by meeting one of two tests: (1) the individual is a bona fide resident of a foreign country, or (2) the individual is physically present in a foreign country for a total of at least 510 full days during any period of 18 consecutive months. The requirement of 510 days (approximately 17 months) in an 18 month consecutive period is flat and unqualified and must be strictly construed. If the artist qualifies under one of these tests, a maximum of $20,000 of foreign income may be excluded from taxable income in any one year. And if the taxpayer has been a bona fide resident of another country (or countries) for an uninterrupted period of 3 years, up to $25,000 may be excluded as long as that bona fide residence outside the United States continues.

The non-resident exemption applies only to earned income; that is, income from wages, commissions, and other forms of compensation for personal services. Royalties are exempt only if the sums received are considered earned income from personal services. An artist who resides in a foreign country may be able to work out an advantageous tax situation by stipulating in his contract that he is to be considered an employee of the royalty user and royalties due him should be in the form of a flat sum, wages, or a commission.

The American artist abroad should also be aware that income tax treaties are in existence between the United States and a number of foreign countries. These treaties are designed to avoid double taxation. Each tax treaty must be examined with care before the artist makes a final decision on its applicability.

PART II

THE COLLECTOR

Chapter 5

PURCHASING ORIGINAL ART

In purchasing a work of art, the collector pays for at least three different things—the quality of the work, the reputation of the artist, and the certainty that the named artist actually created the work. The prominent collector, Richard Rush, urges in his book *Art As An Investment* that the buyer look first for quality. That is sound advice; if the artist loses favor, as have many English landscape and portrait painters for instance, or if it is later proven that the painting had been wrongly attributed to a master when it was the work of a student, what is left but the painting? If it can be treasured for itself, the money spent for the work is not all lost.

If we limited ourselves to *nouveau riche* buying for investment, our audience would be limited indeed—not only because those people are relatively few in number, but because most have attorneys on retainer. The collector buying modestly is probably investing his money in the safest manner. He may be purchasing the works of contemporaries, or of the lesser lights of earlier times. In either event, he is likely to avoid one of the two pitfalls awaiting the unwary collector of expensive works—false attribution. And if the work purchased is pleasing, the modest buyer need not be seriously disturbed by market fluctuations. If prices fall, and they cannot fall too far, the opportunity to enjoy the work is likely to be worth the price, and if they rise, the collector has a windfall.

It is the collector investing thousands of dollars in a single piece of art who must take extreme precautions to insure authenticity, for it is the big names whose works are forged, or purposely copied. The collector who is ready to acquire the work of a great master must never forget the name of Hans van Meegeren, an obscure Dutch artist who, during the days preceding the Second World War, forged and sold paintings that were accepted by well known critics as genuine Vermeers. The discovery that these were forgeries shocked the art world, for several had been purchased for hundreds of thousands of dollars by museums and prominent collectors. These works are now worth only a few hundred dollars, mainly as curiosities. From a legal point of view, it was debatable whether the crime of forgery had been committed by van Meegeren, since he did not imitate anything, but only painted in Vermeer's style and manner. A list of van Meegeren's forgeries is included in Appendix IX.

But forgery is by no means the only source of confusion respecting the attribution and authenticity of old paintings. Copying was once the standard method by which artists taught their apprentices, and to execute a good copy in the days before mechanical reproduction was considered thoroughly respectable. Today, in Europe there are virtual painting factories turning out copies of paintings in the style of well known artists. These copyists are not necessarily dishonest. But despite their best intentions, the attribution given a painting once it is out of their possession is out of their control. The result is that there are doubtless tens of thousands of originally honest copies and probably thousands of intentional forgeries, created by more or less apt pupils, floating around to confuse the critic, the dealer, and the purchaser.

The collector can hardly be too careful in tracing the

authenticity of a work. The first and preferred method is to make an effort to trace the ownership as far back as possible, even to the artist. Frequently, the back of a picture will have customs stamps and other marks of pedigree, including who has owned it and where it has been exhibited. If this information is not available and the work seems worthy of further investigation because of apparent age and quality, a chemical analysis of the pigments can be made. Such an analysis can reveal the age of the pigments, and in some cases it is known whether a given pigment was available to or used by a given artist. Ultra-violet light can show whether a painting has been retouched. An expert can guess from the very brush strokes whether a work is genuine. This kind of research costs money; it is performed by the more important galleries, and it is for this reason that paintings cost more at such a gallery. The purchaser is paying for certain attribution these galleries can often provide.

The person who is knowledgeable in a certain school of art and who buys for quality may well prefer to trust his own judgment on the value of a work; such a person can save money at smaller galleries and auction houses where the facilities for authentication may be non-existent. But it is wise whenever a substantial sum of money is involved, to have a work authenticated by one qualified to do so. A museum official or the art department of a local college may well be able to help. These institutions are often glad to do so, at least partly in the hope that someday the collector will donate works to them.

Auctions.

One of the most common ways to buy and sell art is the public auction. This has long been true. Christie's auction house in London, still going strong, was in business at the time of the American Revolution. Today, the art auction is probably more popular than it has ever been. Since the end of the Second World War, prices for works of art, with some notable exceptions, have risen so rapidly that sales prices at larger auctions are often front page news.

The auction, at least theoretically, provides a means of accurately determining current market values. The "theoretically" must be added, for auctions are subject to manipulation and to waves of emotion. Bidding may be dampened by casting aspersions on authenticity or by art dealers who agree that only one of them will bid for a specific picture. If the one dealer is successful, the picture is then auctioned privately among the participating dealers, and they share the profit made at the second sale. If dealers have a surplus of works by a certain artist, they may bid up the price of a painting being sold at auction to give the impression that the particular artist is gaining in popularity. Waves of enthusiasm among collectors may also raise auction prices well above the level experts would consider reasonable. Still, as a general rule, auction prices are lower than those quoted at important galleries.

The owner of an art work may bid for his own property in the hopes of raising the price. This practice, where it is not made clear that the owner is bidding, is fraudulent. A purchaser may rescind a sale if it is later discovered that the owner or his agents were bidding to force up the price.

LEGAL MECHANICS OF AN AUCTION: In law, an auction is simply a sale with a special method for determining price. There are special rules for auctions related to the bidding mechanism for setting price, but otherwise, auctions are governed by the general laws concerning sales. Unlike statutory copyright legislation, which is national, the law of sales and auctions is local in character. Each state has its own sales and auction laws; there is, however, a general similarity among the states and many have adopted uniform acts drafted by panels of experts.

When an auctioneer puts a work of art up for sale, he is not making an offer to sell it to the highest bidder; it is the bidder who makes the offer. The auctioneer says in effect: "how much am I offered?" And, if he does not hear an offer he considers adequate, he may decline all those tnat are made. When a person responds with a bid that is recognized by the auctioneer, each prior bid is discharged. The last recognized bid is the only outstanding offer; the auctioneer indicates acceptance of the outstanding offer, or bid, by dropping his gavel. Any bidder (offeror) may, by giving notice to the auctioneer, withdraw his bid (offer) before the fall of the gavel. Once the gavel is banged, however, the bidder cannot change his mind; his offer has been accepted and a binding contract has been entered.

The auctioneer's corresponding right to withdraw a property from the sale exists unless the auction is described as "without reserve", or it is otherwise indicated that the goods will be sold to the highest bidder. The right to withdraw property from sale has been used to justify denying a person damages when, after traveling from Africa, to New York to attend an auction, the auction was cancelled. The announcement of an auction, then, is no guarantee to a prospective bidder that an auction will take place. However, the terms of sale and other rules pertaining to the auction which have been advertised must be followed, unless notice is given to the contrary.

Where a sale is without reserve, no lot may be withdrawn after even one bid has been made on it regardless of the auctioner's feeling that the bid price is too low. Lots may be withdrawn, however, before the bidding has begun; consequently, the traveller, frustrated by having the auction cancelled, has no more protection when the auction is without reserve.

The reserve is usually a minimum price below which the auctioneer is not empowered to sell. Sometimes the reserve price may be advertised, although, in practice, the upset price is generally kept secret. Auctioneers prefer not to disclose the minimum price since too low a reserve may dampen the market. The reserve right may also be in the form of permission to the auctioneer to use his discretion in rejecting bids.

In the absence of special conditions of sale, title to the auctioned property passes when the gavel is knocked down and the auctioneer accepts the bid. With the passage of title to the buyer the risk of loss also passes. This means that the buyer bears any subsequent loss by fire or theft, unless otherwise specified by the terms of the auction.

WARRANTIES AT AUCTIONS: The big auction houses, and undoubtedly reputable smaller ones as well, make no warranty of the catalogue description, authenticity, or condition of any paintings offered at auction. Their catalogues will usually set forth the terms and conditions of sale (see Appendix X). Purchasers are normally given the opportunity to examine the works before the auction so that they can determine whether the property is suitable for purchase. There is, however, a code commonly used in catalogue descriptions to indicate the gallery's position concerning attribution: the artist's full name indicates the greatest certainty; last name plus first initial lesser certainty; and the last name alone indicates a serious doubt of authenticity.

When an auctioneer does make a warranty, he or his employer is bound by it. If such warranties are given informally, they are nevertheless enforceable. This is especially true where the auctioneer is or purports to be knowledgeable and well informed, and it is clear that the bidder is not an expert and is relying on the auctioneer's judgment. A catalogue description may also be taken as a warranty where there is no disclaimer. The fact that there have been very few cases in American courts concerning auction warranties on art or antiques suggests that art auctioneers are pretty careful about making claims.

The one thing the auctioneer or his principal clearly warrants is that he has good title to the picture he is selling. This means that no one can come to the buyer at a later date and claim that this piece is really his and the auctioneer had no business selling it. Where there is a defect in title and the auctioneer has revealed the name of the seller to the successful bidder prior to the auction, the purchaser's complaint should be directed to the actual seller. The point is that when the buyer knows the identity of the seller, he is, in effect, relying on the seller to deliver clear title. But where the true seller is not identified, the auctioneer is liable for any failure to pass good title. The auctioneer may also be liable to the buyer if other warranties have been given, although the legal test may be whether the warranty was made within the scope of authority given the auctioneer by the seller. This problem will not affect the right of the buyer to sue for damages or for rescission of the purchase; rather it will only determine who the buyer is able to sue. Where there is any doubt concerning the proper party sue, it is best for the buyer to join both the seller and the auctioneer as joint defendants.

SPECIFIC PERFORMANCE AS A REMEDY FOR FAILURE TO DELIVER: The Anglo-American law has traditionally been divided into two broad categories, law and equity. Equity developed in England in early modern times to provide remedies in situations where the traditional law courts were unable to assist. Law may have been unable to help because it gave no remedy at all, or because it gave an inadequate one. Basically, the only civil remedy at law was the payment of money. On the other hand, equity courts had the power to order people to do things other than to pay money. One equitable remedy is to order people to perform a contract, whereas a court of law could require only the payment of money damages when a contract was not performed.

Traditionally, courts of equity will not order the performance of a contract unless the subject matter of the contract is unique. Therefore, a plaintiff cannot seek an equitable remedy when a painter who had agreed to paint his house refuses to do so. This plaintiff can only go to a court of law to ask for money damages, which is usually the difference between the price settled on in the contested contract and the price the plaintiff had to pay to find someone else to do the job. However, a plaintiff can file an action in equity to request specific performance when a gallery owner who agreed to sell a Rembrandt later changes his mind and refuses to deliver the painting. In this case, a court of equity will act because it is assumed that no money damages will be sufficient to purchase an equivalent to the Rembrandt painting, because there is no substitute for that particular painting. Most, if not all, contracts for the purchase of fine art works are specifically enforceable.

As a general matter there is no longer a distinction between a court of equity and a court of law. However, the traditional equitable remedies are still available only in those circumstances in which the old equity courts would act. The remedy of specific performance, a traditional equitable remedy, would be available in appropriate circumstances regardless of whether the purchase was made at an auction, a gallery, or from a private individual.

DUTY OF AUCTIONEER TO SELLER: The occasion may arise when a collector decides to dispose of some or all of his works by means of an auction. The auctioneer is the owner's agent, subject to the same general rules of agency as is the gallery that sells an artist's works on a commission basis (see pages 6 to 9). There is no problem, however, respecting giving public notice that the agency relationship of an auctioneer is terminated. It is generally recognized that such an agency terminates with the conclusion of the auction.

The auctioneer has the same duty to the owner as the gallery to the artist—to care for the works put in his possession. Both are, as holders of the works, bailees for hire. The bailee for hire (a person paid to hold or handle the goods of another) is bound to exercise what is called ordinary care—the care a person would take of his own property. This rule applies where there is no specific contract detailing the degree of liability assumed by the bailee. A gallery or auction house will prefer, of course, to reduce its own liability as bailee, either by contracting out or by making arrangements for insurance. In dealing with a bailee, an artist or owner should want to clarify the degree of the bailee's liability, and is strongly urged to arrange for either himself or the bailee to purchase adequate insurance coverage.

AUCTIONS AND THE UNIFORM COMMERCIAL CODE: The Uniform Commercial Code, like other uniform state laws, is the product of a commission of experts who draft laws in various fields and urge their adoption by all states. The Uniform Commercial Code has been adopted in a number of states. The Code covers sales, including auctions, negotiable instruments, and other commercial transactions. The sales section is an outgrowth of an earlier Uniform Sales Act, also adopted in a number of states. Uniform laws among the states on commercial matters are of considerable assistance in simplifying interstate commerce.

In most of the states in this country, the laws of contract and commerce are based on the common law of England. Yet, over the years the judges in various states differed in their interpretation of the common law. The uniform acts were designed both to simplify interstate dealings through uniformity and to select from among the decisions of the various states those rulings on specific questions that seemed most desirable. The mechanics of an auction described on Pages 56 to 59, are those provided by the Uniform Commercial Code. Essentially the same approach is followed in states that have not adopted the Code. The same comments could be made respecting the relation of uniform laws of sale and the common law of sales in the various states.

Purchase From A Gallery Or Private Person.

In an auction, price is set by bidding; the terms of sale and applicable warranties are usually settled by the rules for the auction circulated by the auctioneer. In a direct sale, price, warranties and terms of purchase are proper subjects of negotiation, though some galleries may set their terms and leave it to the purchaser simply to accept or reject them. No rules can be given for effective bargaining, other than that the purchaser should keep in mind that he has at least three matters to settle when he does make a direct purchase.

As suggested earlier, price may be contingent on certain other aspects of the deal. For example, a preferential price may be given for cash. Then, too, the price is likely to be higher when dealing with experts willing and able to authenticate a work.

In the majority of cases, well known galleries have sufficient knowledge or sufficient concern with their reputation to be willing to guarantee a work; where that is not true, at least a guaranteed history of ownership may be available. And some galleries, in lieu of, or in addition to other guarantees, will enter into buy-back agreements. Buy-back contracts can be written so as to require the gallery to repay the purchase price or to credit the purchase price or value toward another work whenever the purchaser should want to return the picture; they may also limit the responsibility to buy-back to certain situations, such as when doubt is cast upon authenticity. The terms of the buy-back agreement are also subject to negotiation. In dealing with the established gallery, one is reasonably certain to find one or another of these procedures adopted as a standard method of operation. As long as the adopted method provides reasonable protection, there is probably little point in bargaining for a variation.

Lesser galleries usually sell art more cheaply; they are more interested in rapid turnover and they usually lack facilities for authenticating. They are less likely to be willing to guarantee authenticity. Many reasonable and sometimes very excellent buys may be found in such galleries, but the buyer must be willing to rely upon his own taste and artistic erudition in making a selection.

Despite the fact that the reputable lesser gallery may be reluctant, or unable, to give guarantees on the authenticity of any but contemporary works, warranties may, in some instances, arise more or less unintentionally. In states that have adopted the Uniform Commercial Code, any factual description or assertion, verbal or written, is likely to gain the status of a warranty. Statements of opinion or value, however, usually do not give rise to warranties, though they may where the buyer reasonably relies upon the opinions expressed by the seller; there is reasonable reliance where an amateur or lay person relys upon opinions expressed by a person who holds himself out as an expert.

Warranties that might otherwise come into being respecting possible defects or conditions that could be detected by a surface examination are waived when the purchaser examines the item, or refuses to do so despite a specific request of the seller. Warranties against hidden defects are not waived by the buyer's examination. The reasons behind these rules should be obvious.

Rental Arrangements.

Two types of rental arrangements are widely used. The first is a straight rental agreement where the borrower is expected to return the piece at the end of the rental period. The second is a rental-purchase plan, whereby the rental fee may be applied to the purchase price. The first type is used by institutions with permanent circulating collections; the second is used primarily by galleries or rentals outlets in museums whose main concern is selling to the public.

The rental purchase plan is particularly attractive to buyers who are looking for works of art that they can enjoy. This plan permits the borrower to live with an object for a period of time before making a final commitment to purchase. This arrangement serves much the same function as the buy-back, but is probably more advantageous for the gallery or rental outlet that accepts works of art on consignment.

The rental agreement itself is usually a very simple document (see Appendix XI). The borrower agrees to use the picture for display in his own home only, to respect the common law copyright (see Pages 16 to 18), and to be liable for damage or deterioration resulting from his gross negligence. Insurance against other risks will usually be provided; the borrower should make sure, however, that he understands just what protection is specified in the agreement.

The rental-purchase plan provides, in addition, that the rent paid may be applied toward the purchase price. A two month period seems to be a commonly accepted rental period, although one or more renewals may be permitted. A Chicago gallery, for instance, using the rental-purchase plan allows a two month rental and a two month renewal, the rent for both periods being applicable to the purchase price.

Purchasing From the Artist

With the spread of art fairs, another phenomenon of the post-war art boom, more and more individuals have easy and direct access to practicing artists interested in selling their works. Artists displaying at fairs range from rank amateurs to those having achieved substantial local recognition. The well-established artist, however, is less likely to exhibit for several reasons. First, he may have an exclusive sales arrangement with a gallery; second, he may be executing more ambitious works for which he would have to charge more than the typical art fair patron is prepared to spend; or third, he may simply find an art fair more exhausting and time consuming than it is worth. The mere fact that a recognized artist is less likely to display his work at an art fair should not discourage a collector from buying at a fair. In fact, works of good quality can often be obtained quite reasonably, and there is no middle man or dealer to be compensated. There is, of course, no problem with attribution; the only question is the quality and price of the work. Since a sale is often consummated on the spot, there is little likelihood that problems pertaining to delivery of the piece will arise, unless an arrangement is made to pay for and pick up a work at a later time. About the only type of warranty that might be inferred in this type of a transaction is that the work is done in such manner that it will not immediately fade or disintegrate.

What is true for a purchase at an art fair is true for any direct purchase from an artist. Complications are likely to arise only where works are commissioned or where the artist has an exclusive sales arrangement with a dealer or gallery. If the latter situation arises, a person who purchases from the artist without knowledge of the agency relationship will have no responsibility to reimburse the agent for a commission. It is the artist who will have breached his contract and most probably be subject to a lawsuit for damages. On the other hand, if the purchaser is aware of the artist's contract with a dealer, the purchaser may be subjected to a claim for commissions by the dealer. The prudent buyer should inquire if the artist has such a relationship, but it is not clear just how exhaustive this inquiry must be to claim that a purchase was consummated without knowledge.

Syndications.

With the prices of great masterpieces rising to phenomenal levels, it is not uncommon for groups of art dealers or private investors to purchase these art objects, either for immediate resale or to hold as a long term speculation. Generally, these groups form a syndicate or partnership and each member holds an undivided interest in the property proportional to his respective investment. It may be assumed that persons who enter such agreements are sophisticated art investors and do so with appropriate legal advice.

In a syndicate purchase, the participant is generally approached by a promoter to invest a certain sum of money in return for an undivided interest in the work of art. Where the promoter approaches a great number of prospective investors, there may be some question as to whether the undivided interest is a "security" subject to the provisions of the Securities Act of 1933, as amended. The chief purpose of this Act is to obtain full, fair, and accurate disclosure of the character of securities offered for sale in interstate commerce or through the mails, and to prevent fraud in the sale of securities. If a person is contacted by an art syndicate promoter, he is best advised to check out the deal thoroughly and to consult an attorney before committing himself.

Chapter 6

CUSTOMS

Works of art produced in foreign countries are frequently shipped into the United States. An American museum may be assembling a Renoir exhibition including pieces owned by foreign museums and collectors. A dealer in San Francisco may have purchased a fine piece of sculpture in France with an intention to resell in this country. An American tourist may have taken a liking to a piece of ancient Egyptian art and acquired it for display in his home. Commercial goods brought from one country to another are often subjected to tariff; most countries, however, do not place such duties on works of art. Though the United States has now joined the list of countries that do not levy a tax on works of art, our history in that area is, to say the least, somewhat embarrassing.

The Tariff Act of 1897, reversing earlier policies, had levied a 20% tax on all art works imported into the United States. By 1908, considerable opposition to this legislation had been generated, resulting in the organization of the Free Art League. This organization strove to modify the Tariff Act and gained a partial victory when duties were removed from works of art more than 20 years old, and reduced on other art to 15%. As expected, this compromise was not acceptable to the art world. The argument was advanced that free access to art of the world would cultivate public tastes and increase the demand for the works of American artists. In light of the growth of interest in art, there is little doubt that this was a valid argument. The tariff was attacked, also, for failure to produce the anticipated revenue. Apparently the tax did not protect the American artist from foreign competition; instead it simply discouraged the importation of art into the United States.

The efforts of those individuals advocating the repeal of tariff finally met with success in 1913. In that year the duty was removed from original art works. The real problem was not solved until 1959. The problem was what, for purposes of legislation, is art? The definition of art, written into the legislation, limited the artist to the use of traditional materials, just at a time when new media were being explored. For example, is the collage (the pasting of paper and other items on canvas) a form of art? The customs law, at least, did not recognize it. The law prevented also the free entry of abstract sculpture or constructions.

Faced with problems of deciding what is art in particular cases, customs officials were bound by earlier opinions of our courts which, for certain purposes, had been asked to define art. In an 1892 case, the United States Supreme Court held that not all art was entitled to free entry, but only "free fine arts." The court defined the free fine arts as those "intended solely for ornamental purposes, and including paintings in oil and water, upon canvas, plaster, or other material, and original statuary or marble, stone or bronze." This definition was followed in a number of later cases.

Unfortunately the collage, the piece of abstract painting and sculpture, and the construction did not comply with the judicial definition of art. The courts reasoned that Congress never intended to incorporate all beautiful and artistic objects within the duty-free range of "works of art." Rather the courts decided that "works of art" must be suggestive of natural objects as the artist sees them— *representational* in character. This rule was first successfully contested in 1928 when Constantin Brancusi's "Bird in Flight" was imported into the United States.

The "Bird in Flight" resembled a truncated propeller cast in metal. To the artist its graceful curves interpreted the flight of a bird, but the customs officers disagreed, assessed the article as a "manufacture of metal" and levied a tax on it. The decision to tax was then appealed to the Customs Court. In reversing the decision to tax, the court felt that "under the influence of modern schools of art the opinion previously held has been modified with reference to what is necessary to constitute art within the meaning of the statute." In reaching this decision, the Customs Court listened to the testimony of leading artists, sculptors, critics, and museum officials. In effect, the court took the position that it was not a judicial responsibility to decide what is art, but rather the collector of customs should rely on the opinion of art experts. The *Brancusi* case seemed to be strong authority in favor of abandoning the representational test for determining what qualifies as a work of art.

In spite of the *Brancusi* precedent, the Customs Court in 1934, retreated from its position when faced with the problem of classifying a sculptured glass vase by the French sculpture, Henri Navarre. The court observed that the designs Navarre had molded (after the glass had partially solidified) did not represent anything found in nature. Although three art experts testified that the imported vases were works of art, the court held otherwise, reasoning that these particular vases could have been produced by an artisan as well as by an artist. The court admitted that the method of manufacture and the unique appearance of the vases would certainly appeal to the artistic taste of some people, but that the art style from which these vases derived was merely decorative, and "not such as has always been held to be the practice of the free fine arts." In reaching this decision, the court not only returned to the representational standard as the true criterion for a work of art, but also suggested that the article must not serve a utilitarian purpose.

The effect of the 1934 case was to force the Collector of Customs to make a decision concerning free entry in each individual case. The Collector recognized that a work of fine art had to be representational of something in nature, but found it difficult to avoid a literal interpretation in most cases. His ultimate test was probably based on whether the particular work had a title suggesting that it was supposed to represent something found in nature. Fortunately, Congress recognized the dilemma of the Customs Collector and amended the Tariff Act in 1959 to encompass within the provisions for free entry most forms of artistic expression. These amendments removed many of the judicial precedents and antiquated laws that had previously placed a tax on culture.

Original Works.

The Tariff Act amendments in 1959 modified existing provisions for importing works of the free fine arts. The new legislation contained a "catch-all" clause which empowered the Collector of Customs to admit duty free, in addition to the types of work specifically enumerated, those objects proven to represent "some school, kind or medium of the free fine arts." Such proof may be required by the Collector of Customs from an art expert to establish the status of unprecedented works, of kinds or mediums that are not listed in the Customs schedules.

Besides making the statute open ended, so as not to foreclose from the free entry status the products of new forms or methods of artistic expression, the statute had also to find a means of distinguishing originals and reproductions both in the plastic and graphic fields. The statutory language of the Tariff Act does not envision the free entry of mass produced works of art. On the other hand, it is recognized that "sculpture" is often produced by casting in metal or bronze from artist's models, a method that allows for the production of many castings from one model. In order to prevent the free importation of Eiffel Tower paperweights, for example, the law limits the number of castings that may be entered duty free to ten replicas plus the original model.

Prints and Graphic Art.

Similar problems of categorization arise in the graphic field due to the advances made in techniques for making original prints. According to the Print Council of America, the general requirements for an original print to be considered a work of art are threefold; first, the artist alone must have created the master image in or upon the wood block, stone, or other material used, for the sole purpose of creating a print; second, the artist either makes or directs the production of the print from the material used; and third, the artist accepts and approves the finished print.

There are four major techniques for making original prints—relief, intaglio, lithography, and stencil. Prints made by these methods should be distinguished from mere photomechanical reproductions, which may appear to the uninformed to be original prints. It behooves the purchaser to take great precaution before acquiring a purported original print since the difference in the price commanded by an original print and a reproduction may be substantial. One way to protect a purchase is to request that the dealer state on the invoice that the print purchased is an original print. Obviously, the element of forgery may also be present in purchasing a print and, in the final analysis, the best protection is education and constant exposure to prints.

To qualify for duty free entry into the United States, the Customs regulations specify that an eligible work be printed by hand from plates, stones, or blocks etched, drawn or engraved with hand tools. This requirement eliminates works of art that are produced by photochemical or other mechanical processes. As a general rule, one useful method to distinguish an original print from a reproduction is to locate the signature of the artist and the edition number of the particular print in relation to the number representing the total edition of the series. At the present time there is no limit on the number of original prints that may be entered duty free; the limits are such as may be set by the mechanics of the process and the realities of the market place.

If the declaration to the Customs Bureau states that a print is a reproduction, the importer and anyone charged with his knowledge would be guilty of fraud if the work was later sold as an original print. Should the purchaser wish to authenticate a print before making a purchase, he should ask to examine a copy of the Customs declaration.

Works of Art Produced By an American Artist Residing Temporarily Abroad.

If an American artist temporarily resides abroad and creates a work of art during his visit, he is certainly entitled to bring his art back into this country duty free under the exemptions granted for original works or for original prints. Interestingly though, the revised tariff schedules include as a separate category works of art which are productions of American artists residing temporarily abroad. Moreover, the language of this category is broader in scope than comparable sections since the word "original" is not used in describing the works of art. It would seem, therefore, that the American artist in this circumstance may be permitted to enter duty free more than ten castings, reproductions which are not produced completely by hand, and works that, while artistic in nature, may also have some utilitarian value. Because the apparently broad coverage of this category may be restricted in practice, it would be advisable for the artist to check with the Collector of Customs before shipping into this country, works of his that might not fall under the general heading of "free fine arts."

Antiques.

The collector of antiques should remember that for purposes of gaining a duty free classification, the date of production is the deciding factor. The tariff schedule lists different dates for different classes of objects.

1. Rugs and carpets may enter duty free if produced prior to 1701.
2. Violins, violas, violincellos, and double basses of all sizes may enter duty free if made prior to 1801.
3. Ethnographic objects made in traditional aboriginal styles may enter duty free if produced at least 50 years prior to their date of entry.

4. All other objects may enter duty free if made prior to 1830.

However, if any of the foregoing duty exempted items have been repaired with a substantial amount of additional material within three years prior to the date of importation, a duty is levied upon the value of the repairs at the rate which would apply to the article itself in its repaired condition.

Obviously, other art antiquities may include works admittable duty free under the general definition of works of art. This overlap again raises the problem of the relative coverage of the different schedules.

Stained Glass Windows and Tapestries.

Duty free status for stained glass windows and tapestries depends upon the value and intended use of each item. To be duty free, the glass must be valued at $15 or more per square foot, be designed and produced by or under the direction of a professional artist, and be intended for use in a place of worship. Tapestries must be valued over $20 per square foot and must be fit only for use as wall hangings.

Intended Use.

In addition to tariff exemptions based on the type of work, the law allows exemptions for certain intended uses. For example, where museums and other educational institutions enter what otherwise would be dutiable exhibition material, these articles are placed in a duty free status. In certain situations, a bond must be given by the institution for the payment of lawful duties which may accrue should any of the articles be sold, transferred, or used for a purpose contrary to the provisions of the schedule authorizing duty free admission.

In each case, the schedule classifies each item which may be imported for a duty free use. Thus, the importer must establish to the satisfaction of the Customs Bureau that a certain object, which normally would be subject to a tariff, is to be used for a qualifying purpose.

Export Restrictions.

Before mentioning some general provisions of the United States Customs Laws, the reader should recognize that while our country encourages the entry of original art, many nations control the sale and export of their art. This is done primarily to conserve national treasures. As a result, some nations require that a license be procured prior to exportation, and some nations have even reserved the right of preemption to purchase works of art which may be exported. The collector is best advised to investigate the legal restrictions before purchasing a work of art in a foreign country.

General Customs Provisions.

The Customs laws provide a general duty free allowance which each American resident returning from abroad may claim. On and after October 1, 1965, United States residents will be allowed to bring back with them $100 in duty free merchandise based on the fair retail value, instead of the wholesale value as provided in the previous law. This means that the shipper may include within his $100 general exemption any type or category of taxable art which has been purchased abroad.

Another recent change in the Customs laws eliminates the "to follow" privilege. A resident returning to this country must bring his purchases with him at the time of entry if they are to be included in the $100 exemption. This means that a tourist, who has not used his full $100 exemption, cannot order merchandise to be sent directly to his residence and then include these items in his duty free allowance.

Declaration For Customs.

A work of art, artistic antiquity, original painting, statue, or other object must be declared for examination by a

Customs officer in order to gain a duty free classification. There are standard declaration forms furnished by the Bureau of Customs, to be used for different types of objects or for objects entering under different conditions. Where a work of art is brought into the United States and a duty free status is claimed, the importer must exhibit the invoice covering the particular article, unless the Customs examiner is satisfied that such a statement is not necessary to a proper determination of the facts.

Chapter 7

TAX AND THE COLLECTOR

The art collector must pay taxes on income derived from the sale of art, but, unlike the artist or the dealer who buys and sells art in the ordinary course of business, the collector may be eligible to receive preferential income tax treatment on any profit. In the hands of a collector, a work of art may be a capital asset, the sale of which will be taxed at the capital gains rate. A collector may also have tax questions should he contribute a piece of art to a charitable institution. For the most part, this chapter will be concerned with the tax consequences of a sale or a contribution of art.

Capital Gains on the Sale of Art.

For the individual (non-corporate taxpayer) two alternative preferences are given for income classifiable as long term capital gains—gains from the sale of assets held for more than six months. The tax is on *net* long term capital gains. The problem of what is *net* arises only when a taxpayer also has losses from the sale of short or long term capital assets. Assuming no losses to complicate the situation, the taxpayer may either deduct from his gross income 50% of his capital gains, so that, in effect, he pays the normal tax rate on only one half his gains, or he may elect to pay a straight 25% tax on his capital gains. The first alternative is to be preferred for a person in a lower tax bracket, while the second benefits one in a higher tax bracket. The alternative which results in the greatest saving can be determined by calculating the tax by both methods and comparing the results. The capital gains provisions are, therefore, not exclusively for the advantage of millionaires. Any person selling a capital asset may conserve tax dollars; it is just that the millionaire saves more.

The favorable treatment given the sale of capital assets is justified by more or less reasonable arguments—that it would be unfair to tax fully the income from the sale of an asset held for several years when the income is all realized in one year, and that high taxes on the transfer of assets will discourage the mobility of capital—and by popular feelings that have little or no relation to economic reality—that non-recurring income is somehow not income at all. But, when you come right down to it, neither economic nor accounting analyses provide any basis for the distinction. The boundary line between capital gain and ordinary income has been drawn by considering different types of transactions and granting or denying the favorable treatment for policy reasons or merely because of political pressures.

The result is a law that gives capital gains treatment to gain from sales of what are classed as "capital assets." The problem of deciding what is and what is not to be accorded special treatment is determined by the definition of capital assets. Capital assets are defined by the Internal Revenue Code as all property with certain important exceptions. One exception is property held for sale to customers in the ordinary course of the taxpayer's trade or business. So, the profit from the sale of an art work by an artist or art dealer does not qualify as a capital gain, because, for such a person, an art work does not fall within the definition of a capital asset. A collector, however, who, outside of his normal course of business, buys a painting may report the profit from a sale as a capital gain. This means that when art works are sold at a profit, the seller may choose between the 25% capital gains tax and his normal rate on one-half the gain. The one qualification is that the asset must have been held for at least six consecutive months.

An asset held for less than six months produces what is called a short term capital gain, which is treated differently than the gain on an asset held for more than six months. On the assumption that, in the normal course of events, an art work will be held for more than six months before sale, the treatment of short term capital gains will not be covered in this book. Should a problem arise, the Internal Revenue Service, an accountant, or a lawyer should be consulted.

A person collecting art on a large scale is likely to have other investments which may include stocks, bonds, or real estate. It is worthwhile, therefore, to explain further the statement that the capital gain tax is levied on *net* gain. Net gain is long term capital gain less long term capital losses and less net short term capital losses. Individuals having capital losses pay tax at the preferential basis on the year's capital gain minus capital losses—minus again the excess of short term losses over short term gains.

Gains from the sale or exchange of long term capital assets are treated in the same way whether or not the asset may have been held for the production of income. Losses incurred in selling long term capital assets are, however, treated differently. This is true even though gain from exactly the same kind of transaction would be taxable. As a general rule, losses on the sale or exchange of property are deductible only if income producing property is involved.

Art held by collectors may or may not be held as an investment; that is, to produce income. As a rule, the Internal Revenue Service would probably assume that a collection was not held for investment, and would therefore refuse any deduction claimed for losses on a sale. If a collector chooses to assert that his holdings are for investment in order to deduct losses resulting from sale, the burden of proof respecting his intention is on him. Proving intention, as noted earlier, is likely to be difficult.

The government's refusal to recognize losses on sale of art works means that, where some art works are sold at a gain, others at a loss during a given year, the net capital gain is simply the gain on those works that yielded a profit, not the gain minus the loss. There would be a deductible loss for someone selling art work at a gain only where the loss was on some other property held for the production of income (for example, securities or real estate).

Were it possible to convince the Internal Revenue Service that art works had been held for investment, losses on sales could be deducted from taxable income, with certain limitations. Capital losses can be deducted by an individual if they do not exceed capital gains plus $1,000 (presuming the taxpayer has $1,000 in ordinary income). If there are capital losses left over, they may be carried over by an individual indefinitely and used to offset capital gains plus $1,000 in ordinary income in each succeeding year—until all capital losses have been exhausted.

Donation of Art Works.

The collector, like the artist, may choose to donate a work of art to a charity. As long as the donation is made to a proper organization, the market value of the piece, not its cost, is deductible from the taxpayer's current income. Where a work of art has appreciated in value, the collector gains the advantage of a large deduction without a corresponding outlay of cash. It is more advantageous to the collector to donate the work, rather than to sell it and then contribute the cash proceeds.

Consider, for example, a painting bought for $2,000 and now worth $10,000. If the painting is given to a recognized institution, a charitable deduction in the amount of $10,000 may be claimed. If the painting is sold for $10,000, the collector must pay a capital gains tax, usually 25%, on the realized gain. In this case, the tax on the $8,000 profit would be $2,000. If the donor reduces his contribution accordingly, he will give only $8,000 cash instead of a $10,000 work of art. If the painting is itself donated, not only could the institution later sell the painting for its full value, but the donor would receive a $10,000 charitable deduction, instead of an $8,000 charitable deduction and a $2,000 tax liability.

If, instead, the donor should decide that he wants to recover his initial investment of $2,000 and still make a charitable contribution, he may sell the painting to the charity at his cost and donate the difference between the cost and the market value, reap an $8,000 charitable deduction and also receive a $2,000 refund from the charity. The taxpayer recoups his initial outlay and enjoys a charitable deduction besides.

The least desirable approach, then, is to sell the work and contribute the proceeds. As between the other two methods, donation of the work results in a larger contribution, and sale of the work at cost improves the cash position of the taxpayer while resulting in the same contribution.

VALUING A WORK OF ART: Where a piece of art is sold, its value is usually the selling price. However, where an art work is donated, its value can only be estimated. In recent years, the Internal Revenue Service has looked carefully at the values set on contributed art works. One type of evidence to support a claimed value is the current selling price of comparable works by the same artist. Another form of evidence, and generally the more acceptable, is an appraisal by an experienced and knowledgeable appraiser. As a rule of thumb, tax attorneys advise that three independent appraisals be attached to the donor's tax return to support a valuation. If the valuation is rejected and the taxpayer appeals to the Tax Court, it is advisable that he present the appraiser as a witness. In a recent case, the Tax Court followed the testimony of an appraiser whom it could observe in the courtroom, rather than a paper appraisal whose author was not present.

Evidence of value may also be obtained from an insurance policy. Normally, an insurer will require an appraisal before issuing a policy. This is a precaution taken by the insurer to protect against the over-valuation and the windfall which may result if the work is damaged, destroyed, or stolen. (Insurance protection for a work of art will be discussed in greater detail in the following chapter.)

GIFT OF A FUTURE RIGHT TO POSSESS: Prior to 1964, a collector could give a valuable painting, an expensive piece of sculpture, or an antique to a recognized charity and retain possession of the article during his lifetime. If the charity would take possession after the donor's death, the taxpayer could claim a current income tax deduction for the current value of the future interest, as determined from life expectancy tables acceptable to the Treasury Department. By virtue of a 1964 amendment to the Internal Revenue Code, a donor is no longer eligible for a current charitable deduction if he retains during his lifetime an interest in the donated property. The charitable deduction is considered made when all rights to possession and enjoyment of the property have expired or are held by a person other than the donor.

LIMITATIONS ON CHARITABLE DONATIONS: To qualify for an income tax deduction, a taxpayer's contribution must go to a tax exempt organization mentioned in section 170(c) or section 501(c) of the Internal Revenue Code. Should a donor wish to check on the deductibility of a particular contribution, he will find helpful the Treasury Department's booklet, *"Cumulative List, Organizations Described in Section 170(c) of the Internal Revenue Code of 1954 . . . ,"* which may be purchased from the Superintendent of Documents, Government Printing Office, Washington, D. C. This list is not all inclusive, but if the intended charity appears on the government record, the donor is assured of a deduction.

There is a limit to the percentage of income that can be deducted as a charitable contribution in any one taxable year. The general limitation is 20% of the taxpayer's adjusted gross income. However, the limitation is raised to 30% of adjusted gross income when the additional 10% is donated to certain specially recognized charities. These favored charities include churches, tax exempt schools, hospitals, and medical research organizations, as well as organizations to which the 20% limit applies, but which are supported in great measure by governmental bodies. Private foundations and trusts are not included within the class of contributions eligible for the 30% ceiling, since donations to these foundations will generally come from a few individuals.

If contributions in excess of 30% of adjusted gross income are made in any one taxable year, the excess contributions made to favored charities may be carried over to other years. Contributions to charities subject to the 20% limitation that are in excess of that limitation cannot be carried over into the future. So, if you contribute 20% of your income to 20% limitation organizations and 15% to 30% limit groups, the 5% excess can be charged off in any of the succeeding five years in which contributions are below the maximum. If you contribute 25% of your income to 20% limit groups and 10% to 30% limit groups, the full 30% can be deducted in one year, but there will be no carryover; the 5% excess contributions to 20% limit organizations will be lost.

There is no 20% or 30% limitation on charitable deductions for the fortunate individual whose charitable contributions plus amount of income tax (not including the tax on self employment) exceeds 90% of his income for the current year and for eight of the ten preceding years. Persons who qualify for this tax advantage should adopt a program of donating art on a regularly scheduled basis. The taxpayer should carefully document his income tax return with appropriate appraisals, since the Internal Revenue Service generally audits a taxpayer's return when he has reached the top brackets.

CONTRIBUTIONS IN INSTALLMENTS: Charitable deductions for the full value of art works can be obtained by giving such works in installments. The problem arises where the donor wants to give an art object whose value exceeds his limitation in any one year. If the gift were in the form of cash, the donor need only to arrange to make the contribution in installments in different tax years. But where the contribution is in the form of property, the taxpayer may give fractional ownership interests in the work. Under this plan the donor could work out a system that would call for regular fractional contributions each year up to the amount of the maximum charitable deduction allowable. Because of the newly imposed restrictions on charitable contributions where the donor retains the right of use and enjoyment, it is essential that the art work be transferred to the donee at the outset, otherwise no deduction may be taken.

Conclusion.

Under our tax laws, all taxpayers are entitled to deductions for contributions made to qualifying charities. Under our tax laws there is an added advantage to a business enterprise which purchases art works as decorations and furnishings; these objects become depreciable assets—a major tax advantage. The art collector, individual as well as corporate, is in a unique position not only to gain enjoyment from his art, but also to conserve taxes. Effective planning for these savings generally requires professional advice. The collector would be short-sighted to forego legal assistance before making a charitable donation from his collection.

Chapter 8

INSURANCE

Insurance is important to the collector, the artist, and the dealer. While money will not replace a work of art damaged or destroyed, it will at least reduce or eliminate the concomitant financial loss. For the artist, his works represent an investment of time, and undoubtedly some money. If the works are lost, so is his source of future income, unless that loss is protected by insurance. For the collector, works of art may represent a considerable financial investment. If the property is lost so is a portion of the collector's personal wealth, unless the collector is covered by insurance. For the dealer, his inventory may represent a substantial investment of time and money. If his stock in trade is lost, the continuity of his business may be in jeopardy unless his inventory of art is protected by insurance. Moreover, if the dealer is holding art work on consignment, he is taking the risk that he will be liable to pay the owner for property destroyed while in his possession.

Insurance As Contract.

An insurance policy is a form of contract, subject to the general rules of contract law. It is, however, a special type of agreement known as an "aleatory" contract. The *Concise Oxford Dictionary* defines aleatory as "depending on the throw of a die or on chance." An insurance policy is essentially a bet. The characteristic that distinguishes an aleatory from the usual bilateral contract is that one of the parties to the contract may never have to perform. Whether performance will be necessary depends solely upon the happening of an event that may never occur; the house may not burn down or the painting may not be stolen.

The laws pertaining to aleatory contracts differ in some respects from those respecting the normal bilateral contract. The tendency of the courts is to interpret the promises of each party to an aleatory contract as independent, rather than dependent. If a buyer promises to pay $1,000 for the delivery of an automobile, the buyer's duty to pay is dependent upon the car being delivered. The same contract can be drafted so that the promises are independent. For instance, the buyer promises to pay $1,000 and the seller promises to deliver a car. In that form, the buyer may have to pay regardless of whether the car is delivered, and to gain possession of the car he must go to court. The tendency of our courts, however, is to interpret non-aleatory contracts as if the promises were mutually dependent unless the independence of the promises is made absolutely clear in the agreement. In an insurance policy, however, the insurer's duty to pay upon a loss is normally held to be independent of the insured's duty to pay his premiums. If the insured misses a premium payment and then submits a claim on the policy, unless the contract provides clearly otherwise, the insurance company must pay, though the insurer may have a counterclaim for the delinquent payment.

The Formation of an Insurance Contract.

Insurance is normally sold through agents, some of whom are employees of the particular company and some of whom are independent agents for a number of companies. As a general rule, the agent is not authorized to bind the insurer. Instead, the agent takes the insured's application (offer) and transmits it to the company for consideration. If the company accepts the risk, it issues a policy of insurance that becomes effective upon delivery to the insured. Should the insurer issue a policy and send it to the agent for delivery to the insured, there is some difference of opinion whether that policy is effective and binding before the agent makes delivery to the customer.

There are times, however, when an agent is empowered

to commit the insurer on a temporary basis. This may occur if the insured pays the premium upon the expectation of receiving coverage according to the terms of a specific policy. If the agent accepts the premium, the applicant will generally be insured until the company notifies him that his application has been rejected. It is advisable for the applicant to know whether the agent has the power to commit the insurer.

Subject Matter of the Insurance Contract.

Most insurance of personal property is in the form of insurance protecting all the contents of a house, without itemization. This would appear to be a perfectly satisfactory arrangement where no one item is of special value. But where one or more items are especially valuable, it is advisable that each article be appraised separately and scheduled in the policy. Where several items, each having considerable value, are lumped together, a problem may arise in assigning a specific value to each article. This may best be illustrated by considering the situation in which three valuable paintings are collectively insured for $50,000, and one of the paintings is destroyed. How is the value of that particular painting to be determined for insurance purposes? Or consider the situation where an auction house burns down and the house carries $1,000,000 in insurance. If the paintings in the house are owned by many different collectors, how is a value to be assigned to each painting? Problems of this nature are best avoided by scheduling each item on the master policy and reporting additional items to the insurer as they are acquired.

Types of Insurance Policies.

Art may be insured under a variety of policies. For the casual collector, protection may be gained under a fire insurance policy. Generally fire insurance policies include such phrases as "household furniture," "household goods," "household effects," and "household property." Such phrases have been held to cover a variety of articles, so long as the articles in question have been chiefly associated with the household in their general nature and use. Coverage has been denied where it appeared that the articles in question were not ordinarily associated with the household. By way of illustration, one court held that a Japanese vase was a part of the household furniture, and if not useful, constituted at least ornamental furniture. In purchasing a fire insurance policy, the assured is best advised to read the fine print carefully, and if works of art are not included within the specified coverage to discuss this matter with the agent or the insurance company.

The sophisticated collector, the gallery, the dealer, or the serious artist should purchase insurance specifically designed to protect against the destruction of art. Most companies write a "Fine Arts" policy; premiums for this type of insurance are very reasonable. A "Fine Arts" policy will generally insure against risks of loss or damage to art works which are listed in a schedule attached to the master policy. However, not all risks of loss or damage are insured, and those frequently excluded are:

1. Wear and tear, gradual deterioration, moths, vermin, inherent vice or damage sustained due to and resulting from any repairing, restoration or retouching process;

2. Hostile or warlike action in time of peace or war, any weapon of war employing atomic fission or radioactive force, insurrection or rebellion, seizure or destruction under quarantine or customs regulations, confiscation by order of any government or public authority;

3. Breakage of statuary, marbles, glassware, bric-a-brac, porcelains and similar fragile articles, unless caused by fire, lightning, aircraft, theft and/or attempted theft, tornado, windstorms, flood, earthquake, malicious damage or collision, derailment or overturn of conveyance.

Most Fine Arts policies also stipulate that in the event of total loss of any article or articles which are part of a set, the insurance company will pay the assured the full amount of the value of the set, but the assured must surrender the remaining article or articles of the set to the company.

Most companies will offer automatic protection for a limited period of time for new acquisitions. The consideration for this coverage is generally twofold: first, the assured will pay full premium on the acquisition from the date purchased at pro rata of the policy rate; and second, the assured will report additional items of the nature usually covered by a Fine Arts policy to the company within a specified number of days after the acquisition. If a new acquisition is insured under an after-acquired clause in the policy, most companies limit liability in respect to any one loss or casualty to the actual cash value of the additional item or to a maximum of 25% of the total amount of the policy.

Although an insurer will normally require one or more appraisals before issuing the policy, the assured and the company may fail to agree as to the amount of loss involved. Where this occurs, most Fine Arts policies stipulate that each party may select a competent and disinterested appraiser. The appraisers must then submit their report to an umpire (either appointed by the parties or by a court of competent jurisdiction) for a decision. The decision of the umpire may be appealed to court, but in many cases the matter is settled without going to trial.

The coverage on most Fine Arts policies can be adjusted by use of endorsements. Endorsements are merely attachments which become a part of the master policy, and recite the value and the amount of insurance on each scheduled item. The policy will most likely contain a clause stating that the company will not be liable for more than the amount set opposite the respective articles covered in the endorsement and that such amounts are agreed to be the values of the articles for the purpose of the policy. If a work of art appreciates in value during the effective period of the policy, it is best to so advise the company and have an amended endorsement attached to the master policy. The insurer generally includes a clause in the policy reciting that the entire policy will be void, in order to avoid inflated valuations or the misrepresentation of any material fact concerning the insurance coverage.

Art Works on Exhibition or Loan

There are many instances where a person other than the owner is in possession of a work. A collector may be lending a work for exhibition, he may be selling it through an agent; an artist may be doing the same. And, of course, when in transit a work is usually in the hands of another. The liability for damage to a work in any of these situations is subject to contractual agreement—whether the owner or bailee shall be liable (see discussion at page 60), the type of insurance to be provided, and who is to pay the premium.

The person with a large collection who regularly makes parts of it available to museums and the artist who regularly ships works to galleries will probably want insurance that covers their works at all times, including while in transit and in the hands of others. Those whose pieces seldom, if ever, circulate need not bother with this extra coverage; they may arrange for it on a short term basis if the need arises.

In general, museums and galleries are likely to have blanket insurance policies covering art works they have in their possession. The difficulty of continually relisting and reappraising their exhibits is obvious, but coverage can be extended to a new work by adding endorsements to the blanket policy. The owner of the work should request certification from the insurance company that his piece has been included, by endorsement, in the master policy.

Where blanket coverage seems undesirable, the owner can and should make other arrangements. This is important because most Fine Arts policies do not cover property on the premises of any national or international exhibition unless these premises are specifically described on the policy or by endorsement. The big point with insurance is to be certain what type of coverage is wanted, which will vary from individual to individual, and to make sure that what is needed is, indeed, provided.

Loss or Destruction of Art Work.

If works of art are fully insured under the provisions of an effective policy, the cost of the damage or loss will be borne by the insurance company. This does not mean, however, that the owner of an art work may insure his possession with more than one insurance company and expect to collect the full value of the lost or damaged article for each insurer. Most Fine Arts policies specify that if there is other insurance on the property at the time of loss, the insurer will be liable only in proportion to that insurer's share of all insurance on the property. In this way, insurance companies seek to protect themselves from excessive payouts.

The Internal Revenue Code provides that an individual taxpayer may deduct certain losses not compensated for by insurance or otherwise. The deduction is limited to losses incurred in a trade or business, losses incurred in any transaction entered into for profit, and any losses arising from fire, storm, shipwreck, or other casualty. If the loss involves *business* property, the difference between the value of the property immediately preceding the casualty and its value immediately thereafter may be deducted. A loss to a *personal* asset (not used for business or profit), however, is deductible only to the extent that each such loss exceeds $100. Moreover, there must be a sudden, unexpected, or unusual cause which precipitates the loss, rather than a gradual deterioration. It has been held that damages to personal assets by a flood, a bursting boiler, an act of vandalism, or a "sonic boom" are proper allowances.

In order to substantiate a loss for income tax purposes, the taxpayer must submit evidence in support of the cost or other basis of the property. In one case where the taxpayer could not prove the basis for a painting given to him, he was denied full recovery, but he had spent $100 to have the picture cleaned and prepared for sale; the Tax Court held that since the transaction was entered into for profit, the sum of $100 could be deducted as a loss.

EPILOGUE

I hope that by the time the artist is finished reading this book he is willing to agree with me that the law is fascinating, even if it concerns itself at times with human cupidity, arrogance, and double-dealing. But even if a taste of the law leaves bitter after-effects, it is a form of preventive medicine that the artist will find useful in keeping him out of court, assuring that he is paid, and keeping as friends those with whom he does business.

A letter written by Michelangelo in 1542, which is reproduced below, is proof enough that the legal implications of an artist's activities are not peculiar to the twentieth century.

From Rome,
(October . . . . , 1542)

To Messer Luigi del Riccio.

Messer Luigi, Dear Friend,—Messer Pier Giovanni has been persistently urging me to begin the painting (in the Pauline Chapel). It may readily be seen, however, that this is impossible for the next four to six days, as the plaster is not yet sufficiently dry for me to begin operations. But there is another thing that vexes me far more than the plaster, something that prevents me from living, to say nothing of painting—I mean the delay in drawing up the ratification setting aside the contracts. I feel that I have been cheated, and as a result I am in a state of desperation. I have wrung from my heart 1,400 crowns which would have enabled me to work for seven years, during which I could have made two tombs, let alone one: and I only did so that I might obtain peace and be free to serve the Pope with my whole heart. Now I find myself deprived of the money and face to face with more troubles and anxieties than ever. I did what I did about the money because the Duke (of Urbino) agreed to it, and in order to get the ratification drawn up: now that I have paid the money I cannot obtain the ratification, so that it is easy to guess what all this means without my having to write it down. Enough; it is only what I deserve for having believed in other people for thirty years and for having placed myself freely at their service: painting, sculpture, hard work and too much faith have ruined me, and everything goes from bad to worse. How much better it would have been if in my early days I had been set to make sulphur

93

matches, for then I should not have all this anxiety! I write this to vostra Signoria because, as one who wishes me well and who knows all about the matter and therefore knows the truth, you can inform the Pope what is happening, and then he may perhaps understand that I can not live, much less paint. If I had promised to begin the work, it was in the expectation of receiving the said ratification, which ought to have been given to me a month ago. I will not support this burden any longer, nor will I submit to be abused and called a swindler daily by those who have robbed me of life and honor. Only death or the Pope can save me now from my troubles.

Your Michelagniolo Buonarroti

Reproduced from "Michelangelo,"
translated and edited by Robert W. Carden.
Houghton Mifflin Company (1913).

APPENDIX I

CONTRACTS BETWEEN MATISSE AND BERNHEIM-JEUNE

FIRST CONTRACT 1909-1912

AGREEMENT MATISSE—BERNHEIM

Between Mr. Henri-Matisse (42, route de Clamart at Issyles-Moulineaux, Seine) and Messrs. Bernheim-Jeune (15 rue Richepanse, Paris) the following has been agreed:

ART. I—All pictures of the below-mentioned sizes and intermediate sizes which Mr. Henri-Matisse executes before the fifteenth of September 1912 he agrees to sell to Messrs. Bernheim-Jeune, and they agree to buy them from him, regardless of what the subject is, at the following prices:

Format 50 Fig.—1,875 frs.
40 Fig.—1,650 "
30 Fig.—1,500 "
25 Fig.—1,275 "
20 Fig.—1,125 "
15 Fig.— 900 "
12 Fig.— 750 "
10 Fig.— 600 "
8 Fig.— 525 "
6 Fig.— 450 "

The prices of the pictures of intermediate sizes (formats *"paysage"* and *"marine"* and irregular formats) shall be in proportion to their surface and the above prices.

ART. II—In addition Mr. Henri-Matisse shall receive twenty-five percent of the profit obtained on the sale of the pictures.

ART. III—In the event that Mr. Henri-Matisse sells a certain picture while it is being painted, the difference between the above-mentioned prices and the sales prices shall be shared fifty-fifty by him and Messrs. Bernheim-Jeune.

ART. IV—If Messrs. Bernheim-Jeune leave in storage with Mr. Henri-Matisse a finished painting and he sells this picture directly, the profit shall also be shared fifty-fifty.

ART. V—The sales price of pictures sold by Mr. Henri-Matisse under the conditions outlined in Articles III and IV shall be no less than about double the prices indicated in Article I.

ART. VI—Paintings which Mr. Henri-Matisse himself considers sketches shall not be covered by Article I or the following Articles. Those sketches which he intends to bring into circulation shall, however, be submitted to Messrs. Bernheim-Jeune and a separate arrangement can be made for each one of them. In case no friendly understanding can be worked out, Messrs. Bernheim-Jeune shall have the right but not the obligation to acquire the sketch as outright owners at the rates set forth in Article I.

ART. VII—As soon as Mr. Henri-Matisse has finished a picture he notifies Messrs. Bernheim-Jeune. When delivering a painting he gives them information regarding any negotiations he might have had about the picture.

ART. VIII—Neither Article I nor any of the following Articles is retroactive with respect to pictures which have been commissioned before this agreement, namely: his *Self Portrait*, two canvases of 50, a landscape of 20, two canvases of about 40.

ART. IX—Mr. Henri-Matisse is free to accept, without any compensation being due to Messrs. Bernheim-Jeune, firm orders for portraits or decorations which he receives directly. Decorations will be construed only as paintings of irregular size, the dimensions of which are strictly determined by the architecture of the place where they are to be installed.

ART. X—Messrs. Bernheim-Jeune will receive twenty-five percent on the orders for decorations and portraits which Mr. Henri-Matisse accepts through them as intermediaries.

ART. XI—Upon payment of a forfeiture of 30,000 francs and a simple statement in writing addressed to the other party, each one of the contracting parties has the right at any time to cancel this agreement for the remainder of the time it is to be in force.

ART. XII—In the event that Messrs. Bernheim-Jeune pay to Mr. Matisse the forfeiture of 30,000 francs as set forth in the previous Article, Mr. Henri-Matisse shall lose all claim to the profit ultimately to be derived by Messrs. Bernheim-Jeune from the sale of the pictures which they may have in storage at the time of the above-mentioned payment.

ART. XIII—This agreement has not been registered. If under any circumstances one of the contracting parties finds it advisable to have it registered, this party will assume the costs of registration.

Done in Paris, in two copies, the eighteenth of September 1909.

/s/ Henri-Matisse

SECOND CONTRACT 1912-1915

The second contract, September 18, 1912 to September 15, 1915, is virtually the same as the first except for Article V:

ART. V—The sales price of pictures sold by Mr. Henri-Matisse under the conditions outlined in Article III and IV, shall be no less than about double the prices indicated in Article I. This clause is not reciprocal with regard to Messrs. Bernheim-Jeune, who of course try to sell the pictures of Mr. Henri-Matisse in the best interest of both parties. In exceptional cases they will be free to sell at prices considerably below twice the purchase price pictures which they have offered in vain for a considerable time to collectors; or if the purchaser is another art dealer, or if a reduction in prices might attract new customers to the art of Mr. Henri-Matisse.

THIRD CONTRACT 1917-1920

The third contract was in the form of a letter from Matisse to Bernheim-Jeune, dated Paris, October 19, 1917 (*two* years and more after the expiration of the second contract). The principal paragraphs follow:

I. During the three years beginning September 19, 1917, I agree to sell to you and you agree to buy from me one-half of my production of pictures between the formats 80 to 4 inclusive and at the prices mentioned below:

FORMATS	PRICE	FORMATS	PRICE
80	6,000 frs.	15	2,500 frs.
60	5,000 "	12	2,000 "
50	4,500 "	10	1,800 "
40	4,000 "	8	1,500 "
30	3,500 "	6	1,200 "
25	3,000 "	5	1,000 "
20	2,800 "	4	800 "

II. I agree not to sell to any third party, dealers or collectors, any picture which is in the process of being painted.

III. The division mentioned in Article I shall be handled as follows: I shall advise you each time a pair of canvasses of equal or similar size is ready, and each time we shall draw lots for first choice.

IV. As far as my half of the pictures is concerned I agree not to sell any of them to any other dealers at less than the above prices marked up by thirty percent. If, however, the whole lot is sold the mark-up may be reduced to twenty percent. You, however, agree not to sell to any other dealer any of the paintings in your half at a price which is not at least forty percent above your purchase price.

V. Whether I receive these commissions [for decorations, portraits, easel paintings] directly or through your intervention, they will count toward my half if they fall within the sizes defined in Article I.

From *Matisse: His Art and His Public* by Alfred H. Barr, Jr., Copyright 1951 by the Museum of Modern Art, New York, and reprinted with its permission.

APPENDIX II

ARTISTS EQUITY ASSOCIATION, INC.

New York Chapter   150 Fifth Avenue   New York 11, N.Y.

ARTIST—DEALER FORM OF CONTRACT

1. The   Gallery   (address)   referred to hereafter as "The Gallery" agrees to act as sales representative for referred to hereafter as "The Artist" for a period of   year(s) from date.

2. This contract may be cancelled by either party on written notice after   day (or) after the end of the exhibition season in which the contract is cancelled, to be considered as   date.

COMMISSION

3. The Gallery shall receive   percent of all sales made on its premises.

4. The Gallery shall receive   percent of any portrait, sculpture or mural commissions it gets for the Artist and   percent of any others awarded during the period of the contract.

5. Commissions on purchase prices shall be calculated at   per-cent of the regular gallery list price.

6. The Gallery shall receive   percent of any sales made by the artist personally, without the assistance of the Gallery, provided, however, that no commission shall be paid on any sales referred to in this paragraph, unless the dealer makes sales in the contract year of at least $ for the artist.

7A. The Gallery shall not receive any commissions on royalties, sale of reproduction rights or commercial assignments unless arranged by the Gallery, in which case the commission will be   percent. The Gallery shall receive   percent on works of fine art which it sells for commercial use. It shall be understood that all sales are made exclusive of reproduction rights, and written acknowledgement of that fact shall be obtained from purchaser by the Gallery. Reproduc-tion rights may be specifically purchased with the Artist's written consent in each case.

7B. The Gallery shall not receive commissions on prizes or awards granted to the Artist by art institutions, museums, foundations or a government agency.

8. Materials, installation and foundry costs on sculpture and murals shall be deducted before calculating commissions.

98

JURISDICTION

9. During the period of the contract the Artist shall not contract for any other representation except in the following fields:

.... local representation outside the city in which they Gallery is located

.... foreign countries

.... other (i.e., print galleries)

The Gallery may arrange for representation of the Artist by another agency in any field reserved to it by this contract, but must arrange to pay such agency by splitting its own commission, with no added charge to the Artist.

10. In addition to continuous sales representation during the term of this agreement, work of the Artist will be exhibited in the Gallery:

a) in a one-man show of   weeks duration at least once every years. Said show shall not be at the same time as any other one-man show in the Gallery.

b) at least one work will appear in a permanent exhibition of the Gallery Group.

c) at least one work will be exhibited in all gallery group shows of which there will be at least   every year.

11. Storage space will be provided at the Gallery for at least works.

12. The Artist will receive the following opportunities to co-operate in formulating the policy of the Gallery:

EXPENSES

13. When the Artist has a one-man show at the Gallery, all related costs will be borne by the Gallery.

14. The Gallery will meet expenses of packing and shipping work sent to clients and exhibitions.

15. The Gallery will insure all work in its possession against loss and damage up to   percent of sale price.

FINANCES

16. The Artist and the Gallery will agree in writing on prices for all work in the possession of the Gallery. The Gallery may not accept a lower offer without the Artist's consent in writing.

17. All works are received by the Gallery on consignment and in trust. All sums received by the Gallery on account of works sold are received in trust and the net proceeds, after deduction of commission and expenses agreed to be chargeable to the Artist, shall be immediately deposited in a special trust bank account and there retained until paid out to the Artist.

18A. The Gallery will pay the Artist promptly or before the 15th of each month the amount due him from any sale made in the previous month, regardless of any arrangement the Gallery may make with the client for deferred payment or financing of the sale. The Artist's consent to participate in each case be obtained in writing.

Or . . .

18B. The Gallery will pay the Artist $ per month for the period of the contract, which shall be minimum compensation. The Artist will receive a quarterly statement of his account, and will be paid any excess of Artist's share of sales over his monthly allowance at the end of each year of the contract.

19. The Gallery will set up a welfare fund consisting of   percent on each sale contributed by the Artist and   percent by the Gallery.

20. A Standard Artists Equity receipt will be given the Artist for all work received and he must acknowledge in writing all work returned.

21. Annual statements in writing covering sales, receipts, payments to the Artist and all other matters, together with a list of work on hand, will be furnished by the Gallery, within thirty (30) days after the end of each year of the term hereof. The Gallery shall keep adequate records of all its transactions with respect to each Artists work, which records shall be available for inspection during the regular business hours by the Artist or his representative authorized in writing.

22. Further arrangements:

....

Date

....

For the Gallery

....

for the Artist

....

Witness

100

APPENDIX III

CODE OF ETHICS
OF THE ARTISTS EQUITY ASSOCIATION

In order to establish and build professional and public respect and confidence and to secure to the artist and the society in which he lives the benefits of economic and cultural growth, we establish this code of rights and obligations:

1. To insure high standards of conduct in the practice of the arts, and to contribute fully to the development of our American cultural heritage the creative artist must constantly strive to act so that his aims and integrity are beyond question.

2. Freedom of expression is essential for the practice of the fine arts and is the only climate in which health and growth of creative activity and discovery is possible. The artist should not, in the practice of his profession, be affected by enmities, political or religious strife, or sectarian aesthetic dissension. He should boycott professional activity involving discrimination as to race, creed or ideology.

3. The artist shall endeavor to extend public knowledge of, and respect for his profession through dedication to his work and discouragement of all untrue, unfair and distorted ideas of the role of the artist and the practice of his profession.

4. The artist shall refrain from knowingly injuring or maliciously damaging the professional reputation of work of a fellow artist.

5. He shall assume full responsibility for work completed under his direction, but freely give credit to his technical advisers and assistants.

6. When acting as juror the artist shall constantly maintain the objectivity and seriousness required for this important service, taking into account local practices and instructions from those in charge, and giving each entry as careful consideration as he would expect for his own efforts.

7. When employed as teacher, the artist shall not make exaggerated claims as to his qualifications, nor permit the school or institution in question to do so in his name.

8. The artist shall vigorously oppose vandalism, censorship or destruction of any commissioned work of art, as well as its unauthorized commercial exploitation or defacement.

9. To avoid misunderstanding in dealings with his dealer, agent, or employer, the artist should have a written contract (with the advice of an attorney).

10. The professional artist shall utilize the protection of existing copyright laws. He should claim all fees to which he is entitled for publication and reproduction rights.

11. The artist shall fully assume his responsibility toward his client and shall not misrepresent either the value or performance of his work.

12. Before participating in charity fund-raising sales or auctions, the artist shall assure himself that works will be properly displayed, that established prices will be maintained and that he will receive whatever compensation is agreed upon.

13. The artist shall not enter competitions unless the terms are clearly stated, nor when the fees are contrary to, or below standards currently established. Except in the case of open competition he shall demand compensation for all sketches and models submitted.

14. When executing commercial, theatrical or other design commissions the artist shall familiarize himself with the codes and fair practices of allied trades to avoid misunderstandings in the execution of and remuneration for his work.

15. It is unethical for the artist to undertake a commission for which he knows another artist has been employed until he has notified such other artist and has determined that the original employment has been terminated.

APPENDIX IV

CODE OF FAIR PRACTICE

*As Formulated by the Joint Committee
of the Society of Illustrators, Art Directors
Club, and Artists Guild*

RELATIONS BETWEEN ARTIST AND ART DIRECTOR

1. Dealings between an artist or his agent and an agency or publication should be conducted only through an authorized art director or art buyer.

2. Orders to an artist or agent should be in writing and should include the price, delivery date and a summarized description of the work. In the case of publications, the acceptance of a manuscript by the artist constitutes an order.

3. All changes and additions not due to the fault of the artist or agent should be billed to the purchaser as an additional and separate charge.

4. There should be no charge for revisions made necessary by errors on the part of the artist or his agent.

5. Alterations to artwork should not be made without consulting the artist. Where alterations or revisions are necessary and time permits and where the artist has maintained his usual standard of quality, he should be given the opportunity of making such changes.

6. The artist should notify the buyer of an anticipated delay in delivery. Should the artist fail to keep his contract through unreasonable delay in delivery, or nonconformance with agreed specifications, it should be considered a breach of contract by the artist and should release the buyer from responsibility.

7. Work stopped by a buyer after it has been started should be delivered immediately and billed on the basis of the time and effort expended and expenses incurred.

8. An artist should not be asked to work on speculation. However, work originating with the artist may be marketed on its merit. Such work remains the property of the artist unless paid for.

9. Art contests except for educational or philanthropic purposes are not approved because of their speculative character.

10. There should be no secret rebates, discounts, gifts or bonuses to buyers by the artist or his agent.

11. If the purchase price of artwork is based specifically upon limited use and later this material is used more extensively than originally planned, the artist is to receive adequate additional remuneration.

12. If comprehensives or other preliminary work are subsequently published as finished art, the price should be increased to the satisfaction of artist and buyer.

13. If preliminary drawings or comprehensives are bought from an artist with the intention or possibility that another artist will be assigned to do the finished work, this should be made clear at the time of placing the order.

14. The right of an artist to place his signature upon artwork is subject to agreement between artist and buyer.

15. There should be no plagiarism of any creative artwork.

16. If an artist is specifically requested to produce any artwork during unreasonable working hours, fair additional remuneration should be allowed.

RELATIONS BETWEEN ARTIST AND REPRESENTATIVE

17. An artist entering into an agreement with an agent or studio for exclusive representation should not accept an order from, nor permit his work to be shown by any other agent or studio. Any agreement which is not intended to be exclusive should set forth in writing the exact restrictions agreed upon between the two parties.

18. All illustrative artwork or reproductions submitted as samples to a buyer by artists' agents or art studio representatives should bear the name of the artist or artists responsible for their creation.

19. No agent or studio should continue to show the work of an artist as samples after the termination of their association.

20. After termination of an association between artist and agent, the agent should be entitled to a commission on work already under contract for a period of time not exceeding six months.

21. Original artwork furnished to an agent or submitted to a prospective purchaser shall remain the property of the artist and should be returned to him in good condition.

22. Interpretation of this code shall be in the hands of the Joint Ethics Committee and is subject to changes and additions at the discretion of the parent organizations.

Adopted by the Society of Illustrators, Art Directors Club, and Artists Guild, June 29, 1949; Adopted by the National Society of Art Directors, March 3, 1950.

APPENDIX V

AGREEMENT FOR SALE OF PAINTING, WITH RESERVATION OF COPYRIGHT

AGREEMENT made this .... day of ....,
19......., between .... of the City of ....,
.................................., party of the first part, and ....,
.... of the City of ...., ...,
party of the second part.

WHEREAS, the party of the first part has agreed to sell to the party of the second part a certain painting of which he is the author, and the party of the second part has agreed to purchase the same;

NOW, THEREFORE, in consideration of the mutual promises made herein and other good and valuable consideration, it is mutually agreed:

1. The party of the first part agrees to sell the painting to the party of the second part for the sum of ....
($............................) Dollars, which sum the party of the second part agrees to pay to the party of the first part on delivery thereof.

2. It is further agreed that the exclusive right of reproducing such painting shall remain in the party of the first part notwithstanding its sale to the party of the second part and the copyright in the painting is hereby expressly reserved to the party of the first part, his heirs, executors, administrators and assigns.

3. The party of the second part further agrees to allow party of the first part, his heirs, executors, administrators or assigns, reasonable access to the painting which is the subject of this agreement.

IN WITNESS WHEREOF, the parties hereto have caused this agreement to be duly executed the day and year first written above.

....

....

APPENDIX VI

ASSIGNMENT OF COPYRIGHT

I, JOHN DOE, represent that I am the owner and author of all rights in an original artistic work entitled, "Man With A Guitar" which has been copyrighted solely by me.

In consideration of the sum of $5,000., I hereby assign to REPRODUCTIONS LIMITED, INC. all of my right, title and interest in and to said work and in the copyright thereon, together with the right to secure renewals, reissues and extensions of such copyright.

This assignment shall extend to the full term remaining of the copyright, any renewal or extension thereof.

Dated this .... day of ...., 19........

....
John Doe

Accepted and Approved.
REPRODUCTIONS LIMITED, INC.

By: ....

APPENDIX VII

Chicago, Illinois
Date

R E L E A S E

I hereby consent to the use by you, or by anyone you authorize, for the purpose of advertising or trade, of my name and/or a portrait, picture or photograph of me, or any reproduction of same in any form.

....
John Doe

APPENDIX VIII

THE HANS VAN MEEGEREN FORGERIES

	Dollars	
Vermeer's		
Christ at Emmaus	174,000	Bought in 1937 for the Boymans Museum, Amsterdam, paid for by the State, and the Rembrandt Society.
Christ's Head (a study)	165,000	Bought in 1941, by D. G. van Beuninger and traded in to Hoogendjik, the art dealer, in part payment for The Last Supper.
The Last Supper	480,000	Bought in 1941 by D. G. van Beuningen, of Rotterdam.
Isaac Blessing Jacob	381,000	Bought in 1942 by W. van der Vorm, of Rotterdam.
The Washing of Christ's Feet	390,000	Bought by the Dutch State in 1942.
Christ and the Adultress	495,000	Bought by Herman Goering, 1943.
de Hooch's		
The Card Players	117,000	Bought by D. G. Van Beuningen about 1939.
A Drinking Party	87,000	Bought by W. van der Vorm about 1940.
	$2,289,000	

APPENDIX IX

CONDITIONS OF SALE

The property listed in this catalogue will be offered and sold by Parke-Bernet Galleries, Inc. ("Galleries") as agent for the "Consignor" on the following terms and conditions:

1. All property is sold "as is" and neither the Galleries nor its Consignor makes any warranties or representations of any kind or nature with respect to the property, and in no event shall they be responsible for the correctness of description, genuineness, authorship, attribution, provenience or condition of the property and no statement in the catalogue or made at the sale or elsewhere shall be deemed such a warranty or representation or an assumption of liability. With respect only to Impressionist, Post-Impressionist and modern paintings, drawings and sculpture, if, within twenty-one days after sale of any property the Galleries, in its bset judgment or that of such experts as it may consult, determines that there is valid doubt as to authenticity or attribution, and if the property is returned to the Galleries within that time, the Galleries as agent of the Consignor may rescind that sale of the property and refund the purchase price.

2. The Galleries reserves the right to withdraw any property at any time before actual sale.

3. Unless otherwise announced by the auctioneer at the time of sale, all bids are to be for a single article even though more than one article is included under a numbered item in the catalogue. If, however, all of the articles under a numbered item are either specifically designated by the auctioneer at the time of the sale or designated in the printed catalogue as a "Lot," then bids are to be for the lot irrespective of the number of items. However, in book catalogues, all bids are to be for the lot as numbered, unless specific notification to the contrary is given by the auctioneer at the time of sale.

4. The Galleries reserves the right to reject a bid from any bidder. The highest bidder acknowledged by the auctioneer shall be the purchaser. In the event of any dispute between bidders, the auctioneer shall have absolute discretion either to determine the successful bidder, (in which event his determination shall be final), or to re-offer and resell the article in dispute. If any dispute arises after the sale, the Galleries' sale record shall be conclusive as to who was the purchaser, the amount of the highest bid, and in all other respects.

5. If the auctioneer, in his sole and final discretion, decides that any original bid is not commensurate with the value of the article offered, he may reject the same and withdraw the article from sale.

Or, if the auctioneer, having acknowledged an original bid, decides that any advance thereafter is not of sufficient amount, he may reject the advance.

6. Title will pass to the highest bidder on the fall of the auctioneer's hammer, the risk and responsibility for the property thereafter to be the purchaser's. The name and address of the purchaser of each article or lot shall be given to the Galleries immediately on the conclusion of the sale thereof and payment of the whole purchase price, or such part, thereof as the Galleries may require, shall be made immediately by the purchaser and the property removed from the Galleries' premises at the purchaser's risk and expense. If the foregoing Conditions or any other applicable conditions herein is not complied with, in addition to other remedies available to the Galleries and the Consignor by law, including without limitation the right to hold the purchaser liable for the bid price, the Galleries, at its option, may either (a) cancel the sale, retaining as liquidated damages all payments made by the purchaser or (b) resell the same without notice to the purchaser and for the purchaser's account and risk, either publicly or privately, and in such event the purchaser shall be liable for the payment of any deficiency plus all cost, including warehousing, the expenses of both sales and the Galleries' commission at its regular rates. All property not removed by the purchaser within three days from the date of sale may be sent by the Galleries to a warehouse for the account, risk and expense of the purchaser.

7. Unless the sale is advertised and announced as an unrestricted sale, or as a sale without reserve, the Consignor has reserved the right to bid personally or by agent; and if the Consignor or his agent is the highest bidder, less than full commissions may, under certain defined circumstances, be payable.

8. Items or categories in this catalogue which are subject to the Federal Excise Tax on jewelry, clocks, silver, gold, furs, etc., are designated by an arterisk (*). Unless acquired by a registered dealer for resale, the purchaser will be required to pay in addition to the amount of his bid, the Federal Excise Tax equivalent to 10 per cent ofthe bid. Unless exempt by law from the payment thereof, the purchaser also will be required to pay the New York City Sales Tax of 4 per cent of the bid and all other applicable Federal, State and Local Taxes.

9. The Galleries, without charge for its services, at its discretion and without responsibility for errors, may undertake to make bids on behalf of responsible persons approved by it, including the Consignor, subject to the Conditions of Sale and to such other terms and conditions as it may prescribe.

Reproduced with the permission of
Parke-Bernet Galleries, New York.

APPENDIX X

WASHINGTON GALLERY OF MODERN ART

1503 - 21st Street, N.W.
Washington, D.C.

RENTAL AGREEMENT

Date out ....

Date due ....

To encourage and stimulate a wider public interest and understanding of fine art, the work of art listed below is hereby rented to—

....

Address .... Phone ....

for display on his or her premises for a period of two (2) calendar months.

Artist ....

Title .... Cons. No. ....

Condition of Picture and Frame ....

Rental Fee	Sales Price ....
Sales Tax	Sales Tax ....
Total	Total ....

The rental fee for the object listed above has been paid by the Renter to Washington Gallery of Modern Art. The Renter agrees that if the object is not returned to the Gallery on or before the "date due" specified above, the Renter will pay the Gallery an overdue penalty of $1.00 per day thereafter.

Insurance. Although all objects in the Gallery are insured against certain hazards, the Renter shall be responsible for the safekeeping of the object listed above, and agrees that if loss, damage or deterioration occurs during the rental period immediate notification will be given the Gallery. The Renter shall be liable for any damage or deterioration to the object due ot his gross negligence.

Use. The Renter agrees not to sublet object listed above or to remove it from the specified premises. Renter agrees that said object will not be photographed, sketched or otherwise reproduced.

Term. If at any time during the rental period it should become necessary to recall the object listed above, the Renter agrees to return said object promptly on request. The Renter will then be refunded for the unexpired rental period. Under no other circumstances will any portion of the rental be refunded nor can any substitutions be made.

INDEX

Subject Matter and Persons

Agency, 6-8; 60
Alien artists, income tax on, 49-51
    non-resident, 50-51
    resident, 50
American Arbitration Association, 11
Appraisals, 46, 89
Arbitration, 11
Art Directors Club, 11
Art Fairs, 64-65
Artists Equity Association, 9-11
Artists Guild, 11
Auction, 55-61
    legal mechanics of, 56-58
    specific performance, 59-60
    warranties at, 58-59
Authentication, 54-55; 62
Awards, taxability of, 49

Bailment, 60
Berne Convention, 29
Brancusi, Constantin, 68-69
Buenos Aires Convention, 29-30
Buy-back agreement, 62-63

Charitable contributions, 45-47; 80-84
Collage, 68
Commissions, 1-9; 17
Common Law, 13-14; 16-18; 25
Consideration, 2
Contract, definition of, 2
Copying, 54-55
Copyright, 10, 13-30

acquiring of, 22-24
history of, 13-14
infringement of, 18-19; 24
international, 29-30
notice of, 23-24; 29-30
publication of, 14, 16-18; 24-25; 33-34
renewal of, 14, 24
of reproductions, 22-23
subject matter of, 14-16; 21-22
of titles, 27-28
transfer of, 26-27
Customs Laws, 67-75
    antiques, 72-73
    musical instruments, 72
    original works, 70
    prints and graphic art, 70-72
    rugs and carpets, 72
    stained glass windows, 73
    tapestries, 73

Damages, 4-6; 8, 18, 34, 36, 59-60
da Vinci, Leonardo, 21
Dealers, art, 6, 8, 61-63
Death, 5-6; 17
Declaration for Customs, 74-75
Defamation, 31-39
Disparagement, 32, 37
Donating art, 45-47; 80-84
    gift of future right, 82
    installments, 83-84
    limitations on, 82-83

Endorsement, insurance policy, 89-90
Ethics, Code of, 11
Exclusive sales agreement, 7-8; 64
Exhibition, insurance coverage, 90
Expenses, income tax deductibility of, 47-49
    depreciation, 43, 48-49
    studio, 43, 48
    travel, 48
Export restrictions, 74

Fair comment, 20, 36-37
Fair use, 20-21
Fine Arts, insurance on, 85-91
Foreign artists, income tax on, 49-51
Forgery, 54-55; 71

Galleries, art, 6-8; 61-63

Household effects, 87-88

Imitation, 16, 38-39
Income taxes, 41-47; 51-52; 77-84
    capital gains, 77-80
    charitable contributions, 45-47; 80-84
    foreign income, 51-52
    ordinary income, 77-80
    spreading back, 41-43
    spreading forward, 44-45
Injunction, 18, 33
Insurance, 10, 60, 63, 81, 85-91
Invasion of privacy, 4, 28, 31-34

Libel, 4, 28, 31, 34-36
Loss of art work, insurance on, 91

Matisse, Henri, 9
Mediation, 10-11

Moral Right doctrine, 28
Murals, 4, 46
Museums, 9, 55, 63, 69, 73, 90

Navarre, Henri, 69
Non-copyrightable works, 21-22

Patents, 16
Patron, 2-3; 5
Plagarism, 38-39
Portraits, 4-5
Prizes, taxability of, 49

Release, 4, 33
Rental, 9-10; 63-64
Right of first refusal, 7
Royalties, income from, 44, 52

Satisfaction clauses in contracts, 2-4; 6
Securities Act of 1933, 65
Slander, 32
Society of Illustrators, 11
Statute of Anne, 14
Syndication, 65

Tariff Act, 67, 70

Unfair competition, 27-28; 31, 37-38
Uniform Commercial Code, 61-62
Uniform Sales Act, 61
Unintended reference, 35
Universal Copyright Convention, 29
Unjust enrichment, 5
Utilitarian, 15-16

Valuation, 46, 81-82
van Meegeren, Hans, 54

Warranty, 58-59; 64

112